Crossroads

B2

Englische Handelskorrespondenz und Bürokommunikation

Lehrerhandbuch

Birgit Abegg / Paula White Maier

Hueber Verlag

3. 2. 1. | Die letzten Ziffern
2016 15 14 13 12 | bezeichnen Zahl und Jahr des Druckes.
Alle Drucke dieser Auflage können, da unverändert,
nebeneinander benutzt werden.
1. Auflage

Redaktion: Thomas Bennett-Long, Heike Birner, Kerstin Zülsdorf,
Hueber Verlag, Ismaning
Umschlaggestaltung: Sieveking print & digital, München
Layout und Satz: Sieveking print & digital, München
Druck und Bindung: Auer Buch + Medien GmbH, Donauwörth
Printed in Germany
ISBN 978-3-19-039508-8

INHALT

VORWORT

Crossroads ist ein Kompaktkurs zu dem Thema Handelskorrespondenz und *Business Communication* im Allgemeinen. Das Kurspaket besteht aus einem Lehrbuch mit zwei Audio-CDs, diesem Lehrerhandbuch und einem Online-Service unter www.hueber.de/crossroads.
Der Kurs richtet sich an angehende Fremdsprachenkorrespondent/innen, Fremdsprachenkaufleute, Fremdsprachensekretärinnen und -sekretäre, Kaufmännische Assistenten und Assistentinnen, Wirtschaftsassistenten und -assistentinnen, Europasekretärinnen und –sekretäre und Kaufmännische Auszubildende.
Er ist aber ebenso für Praktiker geeignet, die im Büro täglich mit englischen Briefen, E-Mails und Telefonaten zu tun haben.

Die Inhalte sind auf dem Niveau B2 des Gemeinsamen Europäischen Referenzrahmens für Sprachen angesiedelt und behandeln die wichtigsten Bereiche des Geschäftslebens und den dafür benötigten Wortschatz.
Die realitätsnahen und praxisorientierten Übungen eignen sich nicht nur als ideale Vorbereitung auf die *Zusatzqualifikation Englisch für kaufmännische Auszubildende* bzw. die entsprechende Prüfung für Nicht-Auszubildende, *Fremdsprachen im Beruf (FIB I),* sondern für alle Lernenden, die sich auf die Geschäftskommunikation in englischer Sprache vorbereiten bzw. sich darin zurechtfinden wollen.

Sollen Lernende auf die IHK-Fremdsprachenkorrespondentenprüfung vorbereitet werden, so ist *Crossroads* genau das Richtige für Sie. Der Kurs führt in alle wichtigen betriebswirtschaftlichen Kapitel ein, einschließlich aller vorkommenden Brieftypen, die von Fremdsprachenkorrespondenten/innen beherrscht werden müssen sowie Höflichkeitsformen und Verhaltensweisen im gemeinsamen Umgang miteinander.
Lediglich der Schwerpunkt „Übersetzungen" ist nur geringfügig berücksichtigt, da er den Rahmen dieses Lehrwerks sprengen würde.

Eine Besonderheit von *Crossroads* ist die Verwendung von britischem und amerikanischem Englisch. Je nach Land, mit dem korrespondiert wird, enthält die dazugehörige Korrespondenz das entsprechende Vokabular, schriftlich sowie mündlich. Der Umgang mit beiden Möglichkeiten wird relativ locker gehandhabt, wie dies auch in der heutigen internationalen Berufspraxis unumgänglich ist. Des Weiteren enthält das Lehrwerk Hinweise auf unterschiedliche Vokabeln und deren Gebrauch in den jeweiligen Alltagssituationen. Großer Wert wird auch auf die Förderung der entsprechenden mündlichen Kommunikationsfähigkeit gelegt.

Das vorliegende Lehrerhandbuch ist als schlichter Unterrichtsbegleiter für die Lehrkraft konzipiert und enthält die Lösungen der Kursbuchübungen sowie Erläuterungen und Unterrichtsanregungen zu den einzelnen Kapiteln.
Darüber hinaus bietet dieses Lehrerhandbuch zusätzliche Kopiervorlagen für Fortschrittskontrollen („progress checks"), die flexibel angewendet werden können, z.B. als Kurz- oder Gruppenarbeit für den Unterricht oder als Hausaufgabe. Die dazugehörigen Lösungen finden Sie im Anschluss.
Zusätzliche Musterbriefe und weitere Links finden Sie unter www.hueber.de/crossroads.

Wir hoffen, dass Ihnen dieses Lehrerhandbuch ein hilfreicher Begleiter im Unterricht sein wird und wünschen Ihnen dabei viel Erfolg!

Autorinnen und Verlag

Informationen zur Zusatzqualifikation Englisch für kaufmännische Auszubildende der Industrie- und Handelskammer

Die Zusatzqualifikation Englisch für Kaufmännische Auszubildende wird an einer Vielzahl von Einrichtungen der bundesdeutschen IHKs angeboten. Der DIHK gibt unter www.dihk-bildungs-gmbh.de Informationen über diese Prüfung und veröffentlicht jährlich einen einschlägigen Aufgabenband mit Lösungsvorschlägen. Die Prüfungsordnung ist an jeder IHK erhältlich.

Für Sie als Lehrkraft hier eine kurze Zusammenfassung der **schriftlichen Prüfung**:

a) Geschäftsbrief auf Englisch nach Stichwortangaben auf Deutsch (Bearbeitungszeit: 45 Minuten)
Die Kandidaten/innen erhalten eine Vorlage mit Situation und Aufgabe in Deutsch, nach der sie einen Geschäftsbrief in englischer Sprache schreiben müssen.

b) Kurz gefasste schriftliche Mitteilung nach Stichwortangaben auf Deutsch als Reaktion auf eine englische Vorlage (Bearbeitungszeit: 30 Minuten)
Die Kandidaten/innen erhalten eine Vorlage mit Situation und Aufgabe sowie ein Fax oder eine E-Mail in englischer Sprache, die sie nach Anleitung auf Englisch beantworten müssen.

c) Vermerk auf Deutsch über ein in der Fremdsprache geführtes Gespräch (Bearbeitungszeit: 20 Minuten ausschließlich Aufgabendarbietung)
Den Kandidaten/innen wird ein Telefongespräch in englischer Sprache 2x vorgespielt. Sie dürfen sich Notizen machen. Für die Wiedergabe des Gesprächsinhalts wird ein Vordruck zur Verfügung gestellt. Die deutsche Gesprächsnotiz soll in kurzen ganzen Sätzen in Form eines Memorandums geschrieben werden, wie es in der Praxis in solchen Fällen Verwendung findet.

d) Vermerk auf Deutsch über einen auf Englisch verfassten Geschäftsbrief (Bearbeitungszeit: 30 Minuten)
Die Kandidaten/innen erhalten eine Vorlage mit Situation und Aufgabe sowie ein Schreiben in englischer Sprache, das sie in Form eines Vermerks auf einem beigefügten Vordruck auf Deutsch zusammenfassen sollen. Aus der Zusammenfassung sollen die wichtigsten Inhalte der Mitteilung hervorgehen, so dass jemand, der die englische Sprache nicht versteht, in der Lage ist, diesen Fall zu bearbeiten.

e) Nachweis der Fremdsprachenbeherrschung durch einen Sprachergänzungstest auf Englisch (Bearbeitungszeit: 25 Minuten)
Die Kandidaten/innen erhalten 2 Lückentexte.
In dem ersten Text sind 20 von insgesamt 23 angegebenen Wörtern oder Wendungen in die entsprechenden Lücken einzutragen. In dem zweiten Text

sind die möglichen Lösungen jeweils in 3 Multiple-Choice Angaben „versteckt". Kandidaten/innen müssen die richtige Lösung ankreuzen und/oder in den Text einsetzen.Die Gesamtdauer der schriftlichen Prüfung soll 155 Minuten nicht überschreiten.

In den Teilen a) – d) dürfen die Prüfungsteilnehmer/innen ein allgemeines zweisprachiges Wörterbuch benutzen.

Für jeden schriftlichen Teil erhalten Kandidaten/innen eine Note, die im Zeugnis erscheint.

Das vorliegende Lehrwerk enthält zu allen Prüfungsaufgaben entsprechende Beispiele, anhand derer die Prüfung in geeigneter Weise vorbereitet werden kann.

Für Sie als Lehrkraft hier eine kurze Zusammenfassung der **mündlichen Prüfung:** Die mündliche Prüfung besteht aus zwei Teilen: einem Gespräch auf Englisch, in dem der/die Prüfungsteilnehmer/in nachweisen soll, dass er/sie sich über Alltagsthemen unterhalten kann, sowie einem auf Englisch geführten Telefongespräch allgemein geschäftlicher Natur, das möglichst von einem getrennten Raum aus geführt wird. Für jeden Teil der mündlichen Prüfung erhalten die Kandidaten/innen jeweils eine Note.

Das zuerst geführte Gespräch auf Englisch hat zwei Bestandteile, die jedoch zusammen benotet werden. Der erste Bestandteil befasst sich mit Themen des Ausbildungsbereichs und enthält in der Regel folgende Inhalte:
a) Fragen über Unternehmen und Ausbildung
b) die angebotenen Produkte und/oder Dienstleistungen
c) die von dem/der Kandidaten/in durchlaufenen Abteilungen und schwerpunktmäßige Aufgaben dort
d) Zukunftspläne, Hobbys, Auslandsaufenthalte
e) alle für eine allgemeine Unterhaltung geeigneten Themen, die dem/der Kandidaten/in möglicherweise vertraut sind.

Der zweite Bestandteil des Gesprächs besteht normalerweise aus einem Rollenspiel, bei dem ein Prüfer die Rolle eines englisch sprechenden Besuchers übernimmt und der/die Prüfungsteilnehmer/in den Gastgeber spielen soll. Hierbei wird geprüft, ob er/sie häufig auftretende Alltagssituationen (z.B. Vorstellen, Begrüßen, allgemeine Unterhaltung) sprachlich angemessen bewältigen kann.

Der zweite Teil der mündlichen Prüfung ist ein Telefongespräch auf Englisch, für das die Kandidaten/innen eine ca. 5-minütige Vorbereitungszeit erhalten. Nach Möglichkeit sollte diese Vorbereitung in einem getrennten Raum stattfinden, von wo aus die Kandidaten/innen auch das Telefonat führen können. Für das Telefonat erhalten die Kandidaten/innen eine kurze Situationsbeschreibung mit der Aufgabe auf Deutsch (sechs bis acht Inhaltspunkte) sowie ggf. ein zusätzliches Dokument zur Veranschaulichung der Aufgabe (z.B. einen Prospekt, eine Rechnung, ein Exportdokument). Es wird von den Kandidaten/innen erwartet, dass sie telefonisch die gestellte Aufgabe bewältigen und sich dabei gängiger englischer Telefon-Redewendungen bedienen.

Die Dauer der mündlichen Prüfung sollte 30 Minuten nicht überschreiten.

Das vorliegende Lehrwerk enthält viele Telefongespräche und entsprechende Aufgaben, insbesondere für die schriftliche Zusammenfassung eines Telefonats. Telefonate können jedoch anhand solcher Aufgaben auch geübt werden.

Aufbau des Kurses und der UNITS

Der Kurs ist in 12 Kapitel, „Units", unterteilt, die zentrale Themen im internationalen Geschäftsleben behandeln. Alle Kapitel sind von ihrem Aufbau und der Struktur her gleich.

In Absatz **A Warm-up** finden sich Übungen, die die Lernenden zum Thema hinführen und sich ideal als Sprechanlass und zur Aktivierung des Vorwissens eignen.
Die Absätze **B Business correspondence** und **C Business topics** behandeln wichtige inhaltliche Informationen zu den einzelnen Bereichen im Geschäftsleben und der dazugehörigen Korrespondenz.
In **D Language practice** liegt der Fokus auf bestimmten sprachlichen Besonderheiten des Englischen.
E Listening and speaking skills enthält Übungen zum Hörverständnis sowie **Rollenspiele**, die die Lernenden zum aktiven Üben und Anwenden des neuen Lernstoffs anregen.
Übungen zum Schreiben von Briefen, E-Mails und Faxen befinden sich unter **F Writing practice**.
Im vorletzten Absatz **G Exam preparation** wird getestet, ob die Lernenden die Inhalte der Unit verstanden haben und anwenden können. Die Übungen entsprechen den von der IHK gestellten Anforderungen für die Zusatzqualifikation für Auszubildende und können somit als gezielte Prüfungsvorbereitung genutzt werden. Da nicht in jedem Kapitel alle Prüfungsaufgaben behandelt werden können, werden diese im Laufe des Lehrwerks wechselweise behandelt. Im Zusammenhang mit diesem Absatz bieten sich die in diesem Lehrerhandbuch enthaltenen **Progress Checks** an, welche als zusätzliche Fortschrittskontrollen dienen können.
Konkrete Satzbeispiele auf Englisch und die dazugehörigen deutschen Übersetzungen finden sich unter **H Useful phrases**.

Die in den Lektionen enthaltenen **Vocabulary Tips** mit Übersetzungen sind Hilfen für die jeweilige Lernsituation. Hinweise darauf, wo genau eine Vokabel im Lehrbuch vorkommt, finden sich in den **Vokabellisten** am Ende des Lehrbuchs.

Einen genauen Überblick über die einzelnen Kapitel und deren Abschnitte und Inhalte gibt die **Map of the Book** (→ Lehrbuch: S. 4–8).

Im Anhang finden Sie:

- einen **Layout Guide** mit einer Zusammenfassung aller für das formale Schreiben wichtigen Punkte, inkl. der Unterschiede zwischen der Korrespondenz mit britischen bzw. nordamerikanischen Unternehmen;
- die Transkriptionen der Hörtexte, **Listening Texts**
- **zwei Vokabellisten**, eine nach Kapiteln geordnete Liste und eine alphabetische.

Die **Audiodateien** zu diesem Buch sind auf den ins Buch eingelegten CDs. **CD1** enthält die Hörtexte zu den Übungen aus dem Lehrbuch, **CD2** ist eine vertonte Vokabelliste, die als Wortschatztrainer genutzt werden kann.

Weitere Informationen und Downloads gibt es im **Lehrwerkservice** unter www.hueber.de/crossroads.

UNIT 1
OPEN FOR BUSINESS

Content and skills at a glance:

- international business
- formal and informal styles
- introduction to business letters and emails
- company departments
- greeting visitors
- job titles
- invitations

Einleitung

Unit 1 führt in die Kommunikation im englischsprachigen Geschäftsleben ein. Hierbei werden sowohl britische als auch amerikanische Schreib- und Redeformen berücksichtigt, je nach Land, mit dem korrespondiert wird.
In Teil B werden förmliche und weniger förmliche Texte vorgestellt (Brief und E-Mail) und miteinander verglichen. Die Lernenden sollen erkennen, dass das Schreiben von E-Mails sehr viel ‚lockerer' gehandhabt wird als das Verfassen von offiziellen Geschäftsbriefen. In diesem Zusammenhang ist es wichtig, den Ansprechpartner sowie die genaue Bezeichnung seiner Abteilung und Position zu kennen. Dies wird in Absatz C behandelt.
Absatz D thematisiert die Situation des sich Vorstellens, einschließlich einiger im englischsprachigen Geschäftsleben üblichen Redewendungen und Höflichkeitsformen, deren Anwendung die Lernenden im Anschluss gleich praktisch üben können. Das mündliche Üben geschieht in Teil E, in Form einer Hörverständnisübung und eines Rollenspiels; das Schreiben einer E-Mail finden Sie in Teil F. Der Sprachergänzungstest unter G 20 kann auch für zusätzliche Übungen benutzt werden (z. B. Leseverstehen, Diskussion, Übersetzung).

Die Kopiervorlage für den **Progress Check** finden Sie auf **S. 86** in diesem Buch.

LÖSUNGEN

Die in Klammern stehende Seitenzahl hinter der Übungsnummerierung gibt an, auf welcher Lehrbuch-Seite die Übung zu finden ist.

A1 (S. 9)

Suggested answers; other opinions are possible.

develop a new advertising strategy	both (expensive, but creates modern, fresh ideas)
gain new customers	advantage
increase sales	advantage
obtain special export licences	disadvantage
spend more money on travel	both (expensive, but more international exposure)
translate product descriptions	both (expensive, but translations can be used for other international customers, too)
wait longer for payment	disadvantage

A2 (S. 10)

Suggested answers

Question 1: language barriers, delays in communication, cultural differences

Question 2: learn other languages, find out about cultural differences and try to adapt, use email rather than the phone or traditional mail

B3 (S. 10)

Email: casual, friendly, informal

Letter: formal, polite

B4 (S. 11)

Email	Letter
Less formal language:	*More formal language:*
Dear Celine *(first name)*	Dear Mr Sidorov *(surname)*
... just give me a ring	... please do not hesitate to contact us
Hope to hear from you again soon	We are looking forward to doing business with you in the near future
Kind regards	Yours sincerely
Contractions (what's, I'm, there's)	No contractions
etc.	*etc.*

B5 (S. 11)
Suggested answers: directions, beginning and ending time, eating arrangements, purpose of event, contact information, any necessary preparations

B6 (S. 12)
a. recipient; b. subject line; c. salutation; d. body; e. complimentary close; f. signature block

B7 (S. 13)
a. Tanja; b. Thanks; c. For; d. headquarters; e. coming

C8 (S. 14)
a. quality control; b. customer service; c. human resources; d. purchasing; e. marketing; f. production; g. accounts; h. research and development; i. dispatch; j. sales

C9 (S. 15)
b. sales representative; c. managing director; d. purchasing manager; e. receptionist; f. personnel manager; g. customer service representative; h. accountant

C10 (S. 15)
students' individual answers

D11 (S. 16)
d, a, e, c, b

D12 (S. 16) CD 1 1

b. I am **a** team assistant. (general)
   I am **the** team assistant for the sales department. (specific)
c. May I **take** your coat? OR Shall I **hang up** your coat?
d. **Won't you** sit down? OR Please have a seat.
e. How was your **trip** to our office?
f. I **would** like to introduce Marie Littman, our export manager.

D13 (S. 17)
a. at, in, from, to, on; b. in, to, at, in; c. to, for, of

E14 (S. 17) CD 1 2
a. appointment; b. late; c. have; d. something; e. great; f. Here; g. weather; h. wrong; i. pity; j. this; k. delay; l. terrible; *extra word:* that

E15 (S. 18)
individual student performances

F16 (S. 19)

Dear (*name*),

We are pleased to invite you to the Conference on Recycling Technology, which will be held at the Embassy Hotel located at Tulpenstr. 3 in 20532 Hamburg on 3 March from 9:00 a.m. to 5:00 p.m. The conference schedule is as follows:

9:00 – 9:30	arrival of conference participants, time to socialize
9:30 – 12:30	presentations
12:30 – 2:00	buffet lunch
2:00 – 4:00	interest group meetings
4:00 – 5:00	concluding remarks by Georg Langen, president of EcoSolutions

We have arranged for several experts to give presentations on the latest developments in the recycling field. In addition, the conference will give you an excellent opportunity to network and share ideas with others.

Please let us know if you plan on attending the conference. As soon as we receive your registration, we will send more detailed information. We look forward to seeing you at the conference.

Best regards,

Astrid Hansen
Marketing Manager

F17 (S. 19)

Email

Dear Simon,

Thanks for your visit last week. It was nice to meet you! I hope that you liked the tour, and I'm sure the visit to our company headquarters will be helpful in your job as a sales representative. I hope you'll be very successful!

If you ever have any questions, feel free to call me or send an email anytime.

Best wishes,
Jana

G18 (S. 20)

Email

Dear Richard

Many thanks for your email letting us know that your colleague Sharon Mann will be coming along to the conference. Has Sharon already booked a hotel room? If you like, we would be happy to make a reservation for her.

Also, we would like to ask you to prepare a brief annual report to be presented at the sales meeting.

We are looking forward to seeing you then!

Best regards
Tanja

G19 (S. 20) CD 1 3

Für: Herrn Peter Neumann
Verfasst von: Gabi Kellner **am:** ....
Gesprächspartner/in: John Ferrin, Hopscotch Toys, Einkaufsleiter, San Francisco, USA
Betr.: Interesse an unserer Produktpalette

Herr Ferrin würde Sie gern nächsten Monat in Deutschland treffen. Er hat unsere Website gesehen und interessiert sich für unser Spielzeug.

Hopscotch ist ein junges, schnell wachsendes Unternehmen, das Fachspielzeuggeschäfte in den USA und Kanada beliefert. Besonders interessiert sind sie an pädagogisch wertvollem Spielzeug, das die Kreativität der Kinder fördert. Sie finden unser Holzspielzeug interessant, insbesondere den Safari-Satz mit Löwen und Elefanten und das Zirkus-Set.

Herr Ferrin wird vom 7. bis 12. nächsten Monats in München sein und könnte auch nach Augsburg kommen. Er bittet um Ihren Rückruf unter 001 415 555 44 77.

G20 (S. 21)

The world is open for business

More than ever before, **companies** of all sizes are **entering** the global marketplace. Companies that **export** goods to other countries hope to increase their sales and **profits** and to help their company grow. Companies importing goods from other countries can offer their customers a wider **range** of products, which can **boost** sales figures and make a company **more** successful.

Yet doing business internationally also presents **numerous** challenges. It is very important to find **reliable** business partners who will deliver on schedule and pay their invoices **promptly**. International banks offer various methods of payment to **ensure** that goods are received and paid for. This **minimizes** the risk for both the customer and the supplier. In addition, the shipment of the goods must be **arranged**. Transport can be done by road, by rail, by air, by ship, or by a **combination** of these. In addition, a number of **official** documents must be prepared when exporting goods. If these documents are incomplete or contain mistakes, the shipment can be **delayed**.

Certain "soft skills" are also **important** when doing business internationally. An **awareness** of cultural differences can be helpful when negotiating; businesspeople from some countries tend to be very open and direct, while in other countries interactions are more formal and reserved. Effective communication is the key to overcoming these **challenges** and to developing long-lasting, mutually **beneficial** business relationships.

Words that do not appear in the text: airport, photographs, travel

UNIT 2

GETTING IN CONTACT

Content and skills at a glance:

- writing enquiries
- the marketing mix
- handling phone calls
- market research

Einleitung

In dieser Unit werden schriftliche und mündliche Varianten des Erstkontakts zwischen Käufer und Verkäufer erläutert. Häufig geschieht dies zwanglos durch einen Besuch, ein Telefongespräch oder eine E-Mail.

In konkreteren Fällen bedient man sich einer schriftlichen Anfrage, welche sowohl allgemein als auch spezifisch sein kann. Die allgemeine Anfrage *(general enquiry)* ist meistens kurz und unverbindlich. Bei der spezifischen Anfrage *(specific enquiry)* können schon konkrete Angebote erbeten werden, z. B. für ein Gerät mit genauen Abmessungen oder eine Maschine mit bestimmter Produktionsleistung. Je nach den Bedürfnissen des Fragenden handelt es sich folglich um kürzere oder längere E-Mails, Faxe oder Briefe.

Alle Produkte und Dienstleistungen, die angeboten werden, unterliegen dem Marketing, das in Abschnitt C behandelt wird. Marketing umfasst die Bereiche Marktforschung, Marketing-Mix und den eigentlichen Vertrieb. Der Teilbereich Werbung wird im späteren Verlauf, in *Unit 11 Exhibiting at trade fairs*, noch einmal aufgegriffen und vertieft.

Da die Anweisungen zu G 17 die Adressen für Olivia Feinkost GmbH und Global Gourmet, Inc. nicht enthalten, können diese im Unterricht angegeben werden:
Olivia Feinkost GmbH, Habsburgerstr. 11, 40549 Düsseldorf
Global Gourmet, Inc., 123 Massachusetts Avenue, Boston, MA 02118, U.S.A.
Der Sprachergänzungstext unter G 19 enthält zusätzliche Informationen zum Thema Marktforschung.

Die Kopiervorlage für den **Progress Check** finden Sie auf **S. 87** in diesem Buch.

LÖSUNGEN

A1 (S. 23)
B client, B consumer, B customer, S exporter, B importer, S marketer, B purchaser, S representative, S retailer, S supplier

A2 (S. 23)
Suggested answers: advertisements in newspapers or magazines, websites, trade fairs

B3 (S. 25)
a. 4; b. 2; c. 1; d. 3; e. 6; f. 7; g. 5

B4 (S. 26)
a. T; b. F (Charles Rossitano got Backmeister's address from the German-American Chamber of Commerce in New York.); c. T; d. NM; e. F (Charles Rossitano might order kitchen equipment from Backmeister if the products and terms meet his requirements.)

B5 (S. 28)
a. to meet; b. range; c. high-quality; d. In the meantime; e. keenest; f. ex works; g. consignment; h. collected; i. freight forwarder; j. subsidiary; k. FOB; l. cases

C6 (S. 30)
Product: name; packaging size and type; product appearance; technical specifications
Promotion: advertising, logo, sales promotion, slogan
Price: discounts, price to consumer, production cost, profit margin
Place: export or domestic sales, in shops or online, warehousing and shipping, wholesale or retail

D7 (S. 31)
a. recommended, b. stand, representatives; c. impressed, range; d. advertisement; e. given; *extra word:* network

D8 (S. 31)
Sentences a. and d. are too direct and sound impolite.

D9 (S. 31)
Please send us ...
a. information about your products.
b. an illustrated colour brochure.
c. a current catalogue.
d. a selection of product samples.
e. technical specifications on your model TOM350.

D 10 (S. 32)
a. was visiting; b. mentioned; c. was developing; d. promised; e. went; f. are; g. had; h. hope

E11 (S. 32) CD 1 4
a. a message; b. him call you back; c. leave a message

E12 (S. 33) CD 1 5
Possible questions:
a. How do you spell that?; b. Could you repeat that, please?; c. Would you mind speaking more slowly?; d. Can I repeat that back to make sure it's correct?

E13 (S. 33) CD 1 6
a. Green Line 385/D, Usman Haji, Raja Chulan; b. McGonagall, 113-244-3000, 50, XZT-3; c. Lefebvre, 3698-SFG, j.lefebvre@for-fur.eu

E14 (S. 33)
individual student performances

F15 (S. 34)

Email

Dear Ms Graber

We saw your advertisement in the trade journal *Chinaware* and are particularly interested in your low-cost "Sebastian" line of tableware. Could you please send us an illustrated brochure about this line of tableware as well as a current price list? We would also like to know if the tableware is made of unbreakable material.

Please let us have details of your terms of payment and delivery. How large would our order have to be in order to receive a quantity discount?

Thank you in advance for this information. We look forward to hearing from you soon.

Yours sincerely

Paul Toole

F16 (S. 34)

Email

Dear Sir or Madam

We saw the advertisement about your new software package X9038 on your website and would be very interested in learning more about it. We are an international company and would like to handle all of our accounting with a single software package. Could this program be suitable for us? Is it available in German?

For your information, we are attaching a brochure so you can get an idea of our company and our activities.

Please send us a quotation or contact us at: franz.wagenhuber@nautilus.com.
We look forward to hearing from you soon.

Yours sincerely

Franz Wagenhuber
Purchasing Manager
Nautilus GmbH

G17 (S. 35)

Olivia Feinkost GmbH
Habsburgerstr. 11
40549 Düsseldorf

Global Gourmet, Inc.
123 Massachusetts Avenue
Boston, MA 02118
U.S.A.

September 18, 201_

Inquiry about mustard and barbecue sauces

Dear Sir or Madam:

We saw your advertisement in last month's issue of *Good Food Journal*. Our company is a well-established European importer of gourmet food products from around the world. Since we are planning to expand our range of products, we are interested in products from the US, especially mustard and barbecue sauces.

»

››

Could you please send us a comprehensive catalogue with your price list? If possible, we would also appreciate receiving some product samples.

For more information about our company, please visit our website: olivia-feinkost.eu

Thank you in advance for this information. We are looking forward to hearing from you soon.

Sincerely,

Wanda Frey
Purchasing Manager

G18 (S. 35) CD 1 7

Gesprächsnotiz

Für:	Frau Trier	
Verfasst von:	Laura Lindenthal	**am:** ....
Gesprächspartner/in:	Fred Lange, Luminex Corporation, Ohio, USA, Tel-Nr. 001 216 555 3451	
Betr.:	Interesse an unseren Fahrzeuglampen	

Herr Lange hat Sie letzten Monat auf der MOTREN-Messe in Detroit getroffen und unseren Prospekt über Fahrzeuglampen gesehen. Diese interessieren ihn sehr. Er möchte aber vor einer Bestellung noch einige Informationen haben. Wie hoch sind die Preise? Bekommt er Rabatt auf größere Aufträge? Wie lang sind die Lieferzeiten? Können wir Muster für technische Prüfungen zur Verfügung stellen?

Er bittet um Ihren Anruf morgen zwischen 3:00 und 5:00 Uhr nachmittags deutscher Zeit (unter Berücksichtigung der 6-stündigen Zeitdifferenz!).

G19 (S. 36)

Market Research

Just as consumers get information on products before they decide to purchase a **particular** item, companies need information about their customers when they **evaluate** their range of products or decide to **launch** a new product on the market. The process of **collecting** and analyzing information on customers and products is called market research.

Market research can be used to find out a **wide range** of information. For example, an advertising **agency** might create three **versions** of a television **commercial** for running shoes and ask people in focus groups to discuss and **choose** the one they like the best. A consumer goods company might **survey** people on the street to ask their **opinion** of a brand of toothpaste. Or a specialist market research company might collect sales information about all the **types** of lawn mowers sold in an **entire** country.

Some types of market research **depend** on direct contact with consumers. These include **interviews**, questionnaires, opinion polls, and surveys. Consumers can be asked to answer questions in **person** or contacted by telephone, email or letter. All this is **called** field research.

Once the data have been collected, the market researchers compile and analyze the **responses**. The results of the data are then **presented** to the decision makers (usually upper management), who make decisions **based on** this information. This is called desk research.

words that do not appear in the text: complain, part, welcome

UNIT 3

MAKING OFFERS

Content and skills at a glance:

- refreshing vocabulary
- placing orders in writing and by phone
- types of orders
- Incoterms© 2010
- negotiating effectively

Einleitung

Der klassischen Reihenfolge der Handelskorrespondenz folgend, wird als Antwort auf eine Anfrage ein Angebot geschrieben.

Absatz B erläutert Einzelheiten zu verlangten und unverlangten Angeboten *(solicited/ unsolicited offers)* und bietet abwechslungsreiche Übungen zum Erlernen der wichtigsten Punkte, die bei der Erstellung eines Angebots beachtet werden müssen.
Bezüglich der Vorbehaltsklauseln *(reservation clauses)* empfiehlt es sich, diese im Unterricht gezielt zu thematisieren und zu erläutern. Den Lernenden muss vermittelt werden, dass ein Angebot ohne Vorbehaltsklausel grundsätzlich als bindend für den Verkäufer anzusehen ist. Daher empfiehlt es sich, ggf. einen der angegebenen Sätze hinzuzufügen.

Eines der wichtigsten Kriterien beim Kauf eines Produktes oder einer Dienstleistung ist der Preis sowie die zusätzlichen Kosten (Transport, usw.). Dies wird in C ausführlich besprochen. Unter D werden die verschiedenen Nachlässe und Rabatte behandelt, welche ebenfalls einer näheren Erläuterung im Unterricht bedürfen können.

Absatz E folgt dem Grundsatz ‚Ein Produkt ist so gut wie seine Vermarktung'. Kaum ein Produkt kann man verkaufen, wenn es vorher nicht in irgendeiner Weise attraktiv dargestellt worden ist. Die mündliche Übung E14 bringt hierzu ein Beispiel der *features and benefits*; der Begriff *features* bezieht sich in diesem Fall auf die technischen Merkmale und *benefits* eher auf die Vorteile für den Kunden. Hierzu eignet sich eine Unterrichtsdiskussion zu der Frage: *How can I promote my product or my service in the best possible way?*

Die Kopiervorlage für den **Progress Check** finden Sie auf **S. 88** in diesem Buch.

LÖSUNGEN

A1 (S. 39)
students' individual answers

A2 (S. 40)
a. *possible answers:* friendly, knowledgeable, polite, willing to help, not pushy, open, communicative, honest, etc.; b. – d. *input from students*

B3 (S. 41)
a. So; b. U; c. U; d. So

B4 (S. 41)
a. Sp; b. G; c. Sp; d. G

B5 (S. 41)
a. have learned / learned; b. produces; c. would like; d. am attaching; e. Feel; f. look

B6 (S. 42)
a. Since we have substantial quantities of most of our products in stock, delivery can usually be made immediately on receipt of order.
b. We look forward to welcoming you as a customer soon.
c. As requested, we are enclosing a copy of our current catalogue along with our export price list.
d. Thank you for your enquiry of 6 December about our lightweight luggage.
e. See c.
f. So you can familiarize yourself with our products, we are sending you samples of some of our most popular travel accessories, including a cosmetic bag and a pill box, by separate post.
g. Please refer to the catalogue for information on our terms of payment and delivery.

The sentence "If you have any questions, please do not hesitate to contact us at any time." does not refer to any of the points listed. It is included to encourage contact from the customer and to create goodwill.

Übersetzung des Briefes

Lieber Herr Herrmann,

vielen Dank für Ihre Anfrage vom 6. Dezember über unsere leichtgewichtigen Gepäckstücke. Wie gewünscht fügen wir ein Exemplar unseres aktuellen Katalogs mit unserer Exportpreisliste bei. Schauen Sie bezüglich unserer Zahlungs- und Lieferbedingungen bitte in dem Katalog nach. Da wir von den meisten Produkten größere Mengen auf Lager haben, kann die Lieferung für gewöhnlich sofort nach Auftragserhalt erfolgen.

Damit Sie sich mit unseren Produkten vertraut machen können, schicken wir Ihnen Muster einiger unserer beliebtesten Reisezubehörteile, einschließlich einer Kosmetiktasche und einer Pillendose, mit getrennter Post zu.

Sollten Sie irgendwelche Fragen haben, zögern Sie bitte nicht, uns jederzeit anzusprechen. Wir freuen uns, Sie bald als Kunden begrüßen zu dürfen.

Mit freundlichen Grüßen

Katherine Davis
Verkaufsleiterin

Anlagen

B7 (S. 43)

a. Mr. Armstrong is interested in bicycle helmets.
b. Ms. Hofstetter is sending him a current catalog with this letter. She is also sending Mr. Armstrong a sample of the "Sports Star" bicycle helmet by separate mail.
c. Mr. Armstrong will receive a discount if he orders more than 300 helmets.
d. This offer is valid until the end of July 201_.
e. Mr. Armstrong will have to pay 1/3 of the invoice amount when he places his order, 1/3 as soon as the helmets are delivered, and 1/3 one month after the helmets are delivered. He will have to pay by bank transfer.
f. Ms. Hofstetter promises to handle the order promptly and carefully.

B8 (S. 44)

b. Who are the sender and receiver of this letter? – Peter Neumann of Spiel+Sport is writing this letter to Julia Perkins of Toy World Ltd.
c. What products are listed in the quotation? – The quotation is for toys: wooden train sets, multi-storey car parks and remote-controlled racing cars.
d. How much do the products cost? – The wooden train sets cost €12.50 each, the multi-storey car parks are €15.00 and the remote-controlled racing cars have a unit price of €22.00.
e. How many units is Mr Neumann offering? – Mr Neumann is offering 1,000 wooden train sets, 1,500 multi-storey car parks and 2,000 remote-controlled racing cars.
f. Is there a discount? – Since this is a large order, Mr Neumann will grant a 10% quantity discount.
g. How long is the validity period? – The offer is valid for four weeks.
h. When and how will Ms Perkins have to pay? – She will have to pay by bank transfer to Spiel+Sport's account with the Kommerzialbank in Augsburg. She has to pay half the amount when she places the order and the other half when the customer receives the goods.

C9 (S. 47)

Fixed costs: electricity, permanent staff, rent, roasting machine, website;
Variable costs: nuts, packaging, shipping, spices, sugar

C10 (S. 47)

possible answers: insurance, taxes, advertising, uniforms, cleaning, computers, cash registers, bank fees, office supplies, telephone, fax, training, etc.

D11 (S. 47)

a. introductory discount; b. initial order discount; c. wholesale discount;
d. trade discount; e. quantity discount; f. cash discount

D12 (S. 47)

a. This offer is valid as long as supplies last.
b. This offer is valid until 31 October (BE) / October 31 (AE).
c. This offer is valid for three months.
d. This offer is without engagement.
e. This offer is subject to prior sale.
f. Prices are subject to change.

D13 (S. 48)
a. for, of, about; b. For, of, with, for, to; c. In, of, by; d. at, of; e. of, to; f. with, on, after; g. in; h. by/with, of; i. at, about

E14 (S. 48) CD 1 8
possible answers:
Description 1 focuses on the technical details (power, material, safety, LEDs, etc.) These are the *features* of the sandwich maker.
Description 2 focuses on the *benefits* of the sandwich maker for the person using it: quick meals, healthy snacks, different flavours, attractive appearance, etc.
Effective sales messages can and often do mention features, but benefits are what really attract the attention of the customer.

E15 (S. 49)
students' individual answers

F16 (S. 49)

Email

Dear Ms. Summers:

Thank you very much for your enquiry about our guidebooks for European cities. We are delighted to hear that you are interested in our products. By separate mail we are sending you one copy of each of the guidebooks you are interested in. We are confident that you will be impressed by their high quality.

All of our guidebooks are in stock and are therefore available for immediate delivery. For an initial order we would request payment in advance.

Should you need any further information, please do not hesitate to contact us.
We look forward to receiving your order soon.

Sincerely,

(Your name)
Sales Assistant
Bücherwelt

F17 (S. 50)

Dear Ms Waters

<u>Offer for diver's watches</u>

Many thanks for your enquiry of 10 March about our "Coral Reef" diver's watches. For your information, we are enclosing our current brochure with pictures of all of our models. We are pleased to quote as follows:

10 "Coral Reef" diver's watches at a unit price of €79.95, total price €7,995.00

Please note that we are willing to grant an introductory discount of 5% for initial orders. The price is to be understood FCA Stuttgart Airport. Our terms of payment are 30 days net. We would request payment by bank transfer to our account with the Bavaria Bank, Freiburg.

The delivery period is usually 8 to 10 weeks. However, if you place your order by 15 April we can guarantee a delivery period of 6 weeks.

We hope that this offer meets your expectations and look forward to welcoming you as a new customer.

Yours sincerely
ZEITGEIST GMBH

(Your name)
Export Department

G18 (S. 51)

Rosenbaum KG
Lübecker Str. 120
20457 Hamburg

8 March 201_

Dear Customer

We are writing to let you know that we are planning to reduce our inventory drastically. Since we have done business successfully with you during this past season, we are pleased to make you a special offer. For a limited time, we are offering a special discount of 50% off all the products in the enclosed winter catalogue.

››

»

Delivery can be made immediately from stock. Since this offer is only valid while stocks last, we recommend that you place your order soon. Please use the enclosed order form.

We look forward to receiving your order soon and to doing further business with you.

Yours sincerely

Gabriele Jung
Sales Manager

G19 (S. 52)

Dear Mr Fox

Thank you for your email and for your interest in our sunglasses. As requested, we are enclosing a copy of our illustrated catalogue along with our current export price list. Please refer to the catalogue for information on our terms of payment and delivery.

We would like to point out that we can grant a quantity discount of 10% if the order value is at least €2,500.00.

We are confident that you will be impressed with our products and hope to receive your order soon.

Yours sincerely
DURCHBLICK GmbH

(Your name)
Sales Assistant

G20 (S. 53)

Vermerk über eine geschäftliche Mitteilung

Für:	Frau Marta Siebert	
Verfasst von:	*(Ihr Name)*	**am:** ....
E-Mail von:	barbara.jones@clothesbysmith.co.uk	
Unterzeichner:	Barbara Jones, Einkaufsabteilung	
Datiert:	5. Mai 201_	
Betr.:	Angebot für Kleider und Jeans	

Frau Jones teilt uns mit, dass ihre Firma seit 50 Jahren hochwertige Mode herstellt und dass sie uns mit getrennter Post eine Auswahl von Artikeln ihrer letzten Sommerkollektion schicken.

Sie bietet uns wie folgt an:

1.200 Kleider „Jennifer" (je 300 Stück in den Größen 38, 40, 42, 44), Farbe rot, Stückpreis: 25,00 £, Gesamtpreis: 30.000,00 £
1.500 Damen-Jeans „Patricia" (je 300 Stück in den Größen 36, 38, 40, 42, 44), Farbe Dark-Denim, Stückpreis: 20,00 £, Gesamtpreis: 30.000,00 £.

Die Preise sind drei Monate gültig und verstehen sich EXW Manchester. Wenn wir innerhalb der nächsten zwei Wochen bestellen, erhalten wir 5 % Rabatt auf die Listenpreise.

Die Lieferung erfolgt innerhalb von vier Wochen nach Auftragserhalt. Die Zahlungsbedingung ist: 1/3 bei Auftragserhalt, 1/3 bei Lieferung, 1/3 innerhalb von 30 Tagen nach Lieferung.

UNIT 4
PLACING ORDERS

Content and skills at a glance:

- refreshing vocabulary
- placing orders in writing and by phone
- types of orders
- Incoterms® 2010
- negotiating effectively

Einleitung

Die Erteilung eines Auftrags erfordert größte Sorgfalt, da ein von Käufer und Verkäufer angenommener Auftrag einen bindenden Vertrag darstellt, bei dem beide Seiten Verpflichtungen übernehmen. Es sollte deshalb im Vorfeld genau sichergestellt werden, dass alle vereinbarten Einzelheiten richtig verstanden wurden.

Laut § 433 BGB ist der Verkäufer verpflichtet,

1. dem Käufer den Kaufgegenstand mangelfrei und rechtzeitig zu übergeben (Besitzübergabe),
2. dem Käufer das Eigentum daran zu verschaffen (Übereignung),
3. den Kaufpreis anzunehmen.

Der Käufer ist verpflichtet,

1. den vereinbarten Kaufpreis rechtzeitig zu zahlen,
2. den Kaufgegenstand abzunehmen.

Bezüglich der Lieferung von Waren (Transport) wurden von der *International Chamber of Commerce (ICC)* in Paris sogenannte Incoterms geschaffen, welche die Pflichten, Kosten und Gefahren des Käufers und Verkäufers im Zusammenhang mit der Lieferung regeln. Diese Incoterms werden ca. alle 10 Jahre neu überarbeitet und den Veränderungen im Warenverkehr und den Transporttechniken (Containerverkehr) angepasst.

Eine Auflistung der im Jahr 2010 geänderten Incoterms, die seit Januar 2011 gültig sind, findet sich unter C. Die frühere Unterteilung in 4 Gruppen hat sich in eine Unterteilung in 2 Gruppen wie folgt geändert:

Die Klauseln EXW, FCA, CPT, CIP, DAT, DAP DDP gelten für *alle Transportarten* (auch Schifffahrt), unabhängig davon, ob es sich um eine oder mehrere Transportarten handelt. Sie eignen sich daher besonders für den Containertransport.

Die Klauseln FAS, FOB, CFR, CIF dienen *ausschließlich dem Seeverkehr oder der Binnenschifffahrt*. Der Ort des Gefahrenübergangs ist hierbei immer ein Hafen. Der Gefahrenübergang erfolgt entweder frei Längsseite Schiff im Verschiffungshafen (FAS) oder sobald sich die Ware an Bord des Schiffes im Verschiffungshafen befindet (FOB).

Neu sind die beiden Klauseln DAT und DAP. Bei DAT (geliefert Terminal ...) wird die Ware dem Käufer an einem benannten Terminal am Bestimmungsort/hafen entladen zur Verfügung gestellt. Bei DAP (geliefert benannter Ort ...) wird die Ware dem Käufer am benannten Bestimmungsort entladebereit zur Verfügung gestellt.

Ebenfalls neu ist, dass die Incoterms® 2010 nicht nur international, sondern auch national angewendet werden können. Darüber hinaus können sie, anders als bisher, auch in elektronischer Form festgehalten werden, wenn die Parteien dies vereinbaren.

Mehr Informationen zu den Incoterms in der aktuellsten Version finden Sie auf der Internetseite der International Chamber of Commerce, http://www.icc-deutschland.de, bzw. im Lehrwerkservice unter www.hueber.de/crossroads. Grafische Darstellungen aller Incoterms und des entsprechenden Gefahrenübergangs sind ebenfalls im Internet erhältlich.

Eine gute Erklärung für die Anwendung eines Incoterms ergibt sich in Brief B5. Hier bestellt eine britische Gesellschaft Spielzeug, und zwar einmal für Lieferung UK EXW Augsburg und die gleiche Menge für Lieferung USA FOB Antwerpen. Durch den Transport bis Antwerpen verteuert sich die Ware, die in die USA geliefert wird, da der Verkäufer den Transport der Ware bezahlt, bis sie sich in Antwerpen an Bord befindet. Diese Kosten werden dem Käufer in Rechnung gestellt.

Teil D beschäftigt sich mit dem englischsprachigen Verhandlungsstil. Um Missverständnisse zu vermeiden, sollten die im Englischen vorgezogenen höflichen Strukturen rechtzeitig im Unterricht geübt werden. Unter G 13 gibts es weitere Informationen zu Angeboten, usw.

Die Kopiervorlage für den **Progress Check** finden Sie auf **S. 89** in diesem Buch.

LÖSUNGEN

A1 (S. 57)

possible answers:

<u>furniture:</u> chair, desk, cupboard, bookshelves, bookcase, filing cabinet, conference table, armchair, sofa, coffee table, dining table, dresser, sideboard, chest of drawers, bed, wardrobe, ...; <u>means of transport:</u> car, limousine, bus/coach, subway/underground, train, bicycle, tram, ferry, ship, airplane/aeroplane, ...; <u>office supplies:</u> paper, pencils, pens, toner cartridges, staplers, staples, cello tape, paper clips, folders, notepads, scissors, hole punches, ...

A2 (S. 57)

students' individual answers

B3 (S. 58)

b, f, a, e, c, d

B4 (S. 59)

a. She received an offer, a catalogue and some samples of fabrics.
b. She likes the blankets, but she thinks they are too expensive.
c. Ms Maierhofer will place an order if Ms Hooten lowers the price.
d. *possible answers:* Ms Hooten will agree to offer a 25% wholesale discount.
   or: Ms Hooten will suggest a lower discount.
   or: Ms Hooten will say that she cannot lower the price at all.

B5 (S. 60)

<u>Order for the UK</u>

a. <u>Terms of delivery:</u> EXW Augsburg, meaning that Spiel+Sport will not pay for any of the transport. The customer, Toy World, has to arrange to ship the goods from Augsburg to the UK.
b. <u>Terms of payment:</u> Toy World will transfer 50% of the invoice amount (€35,550) to Spiel+Sport's account as soon as they get the order confirmation from Spiel+Sport. They will pay the remaining amount (€35,500) as soon as the toys arrive in London.

<u>Order for the US</u>

a. <u>Terms of delivery:</u> FOB Antwerp, meaning that Spiel+Sport will arrange and pay for shipping the toys from Augsburg to Antwerp. They will also pay to have the toys loaded on board the ship in Antwerp. After that, Toy World will have to pay the rest of the transport costs to Los Angeles.
b. <u>Terms of payment:</u> Toy World will transfer 50% of the invoice amount (€36,478.50) to Spiel+Sport's account as soon as they get the order confirmation from Spiel+Sport. They will pay the remaining amount(€36,478.50) as soon as the toys arrive in Los Angeles.

B6 (S. 62)

a. by; b. with; c. at; d. on; e. to; f. in; g. on; h. by; i. of; j. at

C7 (S. 65)

b. DAT Dublin Terminal; c. CFR New York; d. DAP Vancouver Airport; e. CIP Stuttgart Railway Station; f. DDP St Petersburg; g. EXW Cologne; h. FAS Antwerp; i. CIF New Delhi

D8 (S. 67) CD 1 **9**

a. 4; b. 2; c. 5; d. 6; e. 1; f. 3

D9 (S. 67) CD 1 **10**

possible answers:

a. It seems rather difficult for you to understand what we need.
b. We would appreciate it if you could give us a larger discount.
c. Your products seem quite expensive.
d. Actually, that's not really a very good idea.
e. It seems that we won't be able to deliver your order on time.
   There will be a slight delay.
f. We were hoping that you might be able to give us some more time.
g. I'm afraid that this is a slight problem for us.
h. Unfortunately we can't accept this offer.

E10 (S. 68) CD 1 **11**

a. Charles Rossitano is calling Tanja Buchner.
b. Charles Rossitano works for Kitchen Specialists in New York.
   Tanja Buchner is with Backmeister GmbH.
c. Charles Rossitano is interested in ordering two products, the DoughMaster 3000 industrial mixer and the AromaBake 45 industrial oven. He would like ten of each. But he also has a number of questions about delivery time, discounts etc.
d. 20%.
e. Tanja Buchner says she will talk to her boss, Mr. Wunderlich, and ask him to ring Charles Rossitano.

E11 (S. 68)

individual student performances

F12 (S. 70)

Dear Mr Present

Thank you for your offer along with the catalogue and the product samples. As we are particularly impressed with the excellent quality of your umbrellas, we are pleased to place the following order with you:

1000 umbrellas, model "Rainbow", at a price of €10 per unit, less 5% initial order discount, total price €9,500

The price is to be understood CFR Dublin. As agreed, payment will be made by bank transfer within two weeks of the invoice date. We are planning to use these umbrellas as a promotional gift at a trade fair in October. For this reason, complete delivery by the end of September at the latest is absolutely essential. We reserve the right to return the goods at your risk and expense if the consignment is late.

Could you send us a confirmation of our order as soon as possible? We look forward to receiving the umbrellas in time and to doing further business with you.

Yours sincerely

Theresa Kober
Purchasing Manager

G13 (S. 71)

1. states; 2. will; 3. services; 4. on; 5. because; 6. which; 7. Whether; 8. on; 9. clause; 10. needs; 11. if; 12. Should; 13. more; 14. than; 15. will; 16. accept; 17. which; 18. region; 19. customary; 20. often; 21. on; 22. such; 23. some; 24. them; 25. great; 26. in; 27. many; 28. be; 29. together; 30. other

G14 (S. 72)

Email

From: wanda.frey@olivia-feinkost.de
To: harry.taylor@globalgourmet.com
Sent: December 10, 201_
Re: Order No. 30914

Dear Mr. Taylor,

Thank you for sending us the samples so quickly. We are impressed with their quality and are pleased to place the following order with you:

300 jars of "Spicy Sweet Mustard", 150 g each, at a unit price of $ 2.50, total price $ 750
400 bottles of "Mother's Delight" barbecue sauce, 250 g each, at a unit price of $ 1.70, total price $ 680

The total price of this order is $ 1,430 including packaging. We would like to have the goods delivered DAP Logan International Airport in Boston and are prepared to pay the additional amount of 10%, or $ 143. The resulting total price amounts to $ 1,573.

Please accept this email as our order as long as the total price does not go over this amount. We look forward to receiving your confirmation by email.

Best regards,

Wanda Frey

G15 (S. 73) CD 1 11

Für:	Jens Wunderlich	
Verfasst von:	Tanja Buchner	**am:** ....
Gesprächspartner:	Charles Rossitano, New York, U.S.A.	
Betr.:	Unser Angebot über Rührmaschinen und Backöfen für Großbäckereien	

Heute nahm ich den Anruf von Herrn Rossitano entgegen, der den Empfang unserer Prospekte bestätigt. Bevor er uns einen Auftrag erteilt, möchte er folgende Fragen klären:

1. Er hat vor, 10 Stück DoughMaster 3000 Industriemixer, Produkt-Nr. 5768-32, zu bestellen. Laut Preisliste kosten die 1.600 € pro Stück. Stimmt das noch? Ich habe ihm das bestätigt.
2. Wie lange ist die Lieferzeit? Haben wir die auf Lager? Ich sagte ihm, dass die Lieferzeit für dieses Produkt ab Auftragseingang 4 Wochen beträgt.
3. Er möchte auch 10 AromaBake 45 Industrieöfen, Produkt-Nr. 7002-78, zum Einzelpreis von 2.300 € bestellen. Wie lange ist hier die Lieferzeit? Ich habe gesagt, dass wir die sofort ab Lager liefern können.
4. Herr Rossitano geht also von einem Gesamtpreis von 39.000 € aus und möchte darauf natürlich einen Mengenrabatt haben. Ich habe gesagt, dass ich hierfür mit Ihnen Rücksprache halten muss, ihm aber 15% in Aussicht gestellt. Er möchte 20% haben.

Er wird die Bestellung erteilen, sobald er von uns hört. Sie möchten ihn bitte unter 001-718-555-0991, Nebenstelle 103 anrufen.

UNIT 5

DEALING WITH ORDERS

Content and skills at a glance:

- differentiating between American and British English
- confirming orders
- writing counteroffers
- enquiring about delivery

Einleitung

Die Einstiegsübung thematisiert die Unterschiede zwischen britischem und amerikanischem Englisch. Die aufgeführte Tabelle kann, je nach Interesse und Bedarf im Unterricht, mit Hilfe einer Internetrecherche von den Lernenden beliebig ergänzt werden.

In der allgemeinen Handelskette folgt dem Auftrag gewöhnlich die Auftragsbestätigung. Es empfiehlt sich immer, eine solche auszustellen, wenn auch nur in kurzer Form. Sie gibt dem Lieferanten die Sicherheit, dass er nunmehr mit der Produktion der Ware oder der Vorbereitung der Dienstleistung beginnen kann. Wie dies vor sich geht, wird unter B beschrieben.

Unter C erfolgt die Einführung in die Zahlungsbedingungen *(terms of payment)* und Zahlungsarten *(methods of payment)*.
Der Vollständigkeit halber sind die gängigsten Zahlungsarten aufgeführt, wobei der Wechsel *(bill of exchange B/E)* und das Akkreditiv *(letter of credit L/C)* an dieser Stelle nur in Kurzform behandelt werden. Da der Wechsel an Bedeutung abnimmt, wird in diesem Buch auf die Erwähnung der Sicht- und Nachsichtwechsel verzichtet. Das Akkreditiv wird nur in seiner einfachsten Form vorgestellt, um den Lernenden nicht zu überfordern.
Auch die im Außenhandel noch verwendeten Zahlungsbedingungen Kasse gegen Dokumente *(documents against payment D/P)* und Dokumente gegen Akzept *(documents against acceptance D/A)* werden nur kurz erwähnt, da das Lehrwerk kein großes Exportgeschäft thematisiert.

Der Sprachergänzungstest unter G 15 behandelt das Thema Geldautomaten und wie diese als Mittel zum Geldabheben oder für weitere Bankdienstleistungen in Anspruch genommen werden können.

Die Kopiervorlage für den **Progress Check** finden Sie auf **S. 90** in diesem Buch.

LÖSUNGEN

A1 (S. 76)

British English	American English
catalogue	catalog
fortnight	**two weeks**
lift	elevator
lorry	**truck**
mobile phone	cell phone
per cent	**percent**
petrol	gas
dialling code	**area code**
engaged (phone line)	busy (phone line)

A2 (S. 77)

possible answers:

behaviour/behavior, favourite/favorite, honour/honor, humour/humor, labour/labor, criticise/criticize, organise/organize, memorise/memorize, enrol/enroll, fulfil/fulfill, skilful/skillful, litre/liter, metre/meter, theatre/theater, judgement/judgment, defence/defense, licence/license, aeroplane/airplane, aluminium/aluminum, jewellery/jewelry, pyjamas/pajamas, grey/gray, programme/program, plough/plow, tyre/tire

B3 (S. 78)

a. The price for the US consignment is higher than the price for the UK consignment because the shipping costs for the US consignment are higher.

b. The consignment for the US is going to be loaded on board a ship, which will take the toys to Los Angeles.

c. First instalment: €72,028.50 (half of the UK amount, which is €35,550.00, plus half of the US amount, which is €36,478.50)
Second instalment: €35,550.00 (the remaining 50% of the UK amount)
Third instalment: €36,478.50 (the remaining 50% of the US amount)

d. He wants to be able to let someone in the Los Angeles office know when the ship will be arriving.

e. He promises that Spiel+Sport will give a lot of attention to the order so that nothing goes wrong and that Toy World (the customer) will be very happy with the goods and the delivery.

B4 (S. 80)

possible answer: Mr Mendelson called Buchexport Thomas GmbH to order some dictionaries. Rita Sievertson is now writing back to confirm the order. He ordered 100 TechnoDict 2020 multilingual technical dictionaries (English / Spanish / French / German). Each one costs 79 euros, so the total is 7,900 euros. The term of delivery is EXW (ex works) Hanover. Mr Mendelson will have to pay by bank transfer when he receives the dictionaries. Wordsmith Publishing is working on getting the order ready and will send it in three days or less. They promise to send the order quickly and to handle it carefully.

B5 (S. 81)

b. regret; c. trust; d. at the moment; e. let us have your instructions;
f. stopped manufacturing; g. see

B6 (S. 82)

a. up; b. for; c. of; d. to; e. with; f. For; g. of; h. to; i. from; j. with

C7 (S. 85)

a. S; if the buyer pays in advance, the seller has no risk.
b. B; the buyer can wait until the goods arrive before paying. The seller has no guarantee that payment will be made.
c. B; the buyer has a period of 30 days to pay and can deduct 2% of the invoice amount if payment is made within 10 days.
d. S + B; payment by bank transfer is fast and relatively inexpensive compared to other methods of payment.
e. S + B; the seller gets a type of guarantee that payment will be made and the buyer has 60 days in which to pay.
f. S + B; the seller gets part of the money right away but the buyer has time to check and test the goods before making the final payment.
g. S + B; this is the most secure method of handling payment because the shipping documents (=the goods) and the money are kept by the banks until everything has been checked and is in order.

D8 (S. 85)

b. would like to; c. say you; d. hold; e. made; f. delivered

D9 (S. 85)

possible answers:

a. Many thanks for your order no. 78896 dated 15 October (BE) / October 15 (AE).
b. We are pleased to confirm that the quantity you requested is in stock and can be dispatched shortly.
c. Unfortunately the article you ordered is unavailable at the moment.
We will not be able to deliver it until two weeks from now.

d. We are prepared to grant the quantity discount of 15% you requested. However, this is only valid for your current order.
e. Since you are a new customer, we would request payment in advance.
f. Our terms of payment are 10 days 2% or 30 days net.
g. We hope to do business with you again in future (BE) / in the future (AE).

E10 (S. 86) CD 1 12

a. calling; b. business; c. slight; d. actually; e. typing; f. happen; g. mix-up; h. speed; i. stock; j. less; k. understanding; l. hoping; *extra word:* supplier

E11 (S. 87)

individual student performances

F12 (S. 88)

Dear Mr. Rossitano:

Thank you for your order, which we received by telephone and then by email. We are pleased to confirm the details of the order as follows:

Qty.	Product	Number	Unit Price	Total	
10	DoughMaster 3000 industrial mixers	5678-32	€1,600.00	€16,000.00	
10	AromaBake 45 industrial ovens	7002-78	€2,300.00	€23,000.00	
				€39,000.00	Subtotal
				- 7,800.00	less 20% discount
				€31,200.00	**Total**

As we discussed, the delivery period for these products is six weeks. The price is to be understood FOB Bremerhaven. Payment will be made 1/3 with order, 1/3 on receipt of the goods, and 1/3 within 30 days after receipt of the goods.

You may rest assured that your order will be executed promptly and carefully. We look forward to the pleasure of doing business with you again.

Sincerely,
Backmeister GmbH

Jens Wunderlich
Sales Manager

G13 (S. 89)

Atlas AG
Bergheimer Str. 40
47166 Duisburg

Johnson Machinery Ltd
Midland House
23 Hunt Street
London EC3 2BE
UK

(Date)

Dear Sir or Madam

Confirmation of order

Many thanks for your order for our high-performance printer, model no. 309847 3EX, which we are pleased to confirm.

We would like to point out that the price of €5,400.00 was quoted EXW Duisburg. Since you have now requested delivery DAT Dover, we will need to add the transport costs to the terminal in Dover, including the unloading charges and the insurance against risk. This will result in an additional charge of €650.00. Please confirm your acceptance of the total price of €6,050.00. All of the other terms will remain the same.

Thank you again for choosing to place your order with us. We are confident that you will be very satisfied with the quality of your new printer and look forward to doing business with you again.

Yours sincerely
Atlas AG

Günther Gerwin
Managing Director

G14 (S. 90) CD 1 13

Für: Herrn Hans Schmied
Verfasst von: Lukas Jost **am:** ....
Gesprächspartner/in: Herr Terry Cullen, The Cutting Edge, Atlanta, Georgia, U.S.A.
Betr.: Auftrag über 150 Gartenscheren Art.-Nr. 89099 und 200 Kinderscheren für Linkshänder Art.Nr. 72012

Herr Cullen hatte sich bei seinem 1. Auftrag nach einem alten Katalog gerichtet und bestellt jetzt die obigen Mengen und Artikel-Nummern. Ich bestätigte ihm einen Stückpreis von 19 € für die Gartenscheren und einen von 8 € für die Kinderscheren für Linkshänder. Er möchte einen Nachlass von 10 % auf die Gesamtsumme, den ich ihm zugesagt habe, da die Kinderscheren momentan nicht auf Lager sind.

Lieferzeit: Gartenscheren ab Lager, Kinderscheren sobald verfügbar.
Lieferbedingung: Ab Werk
Zahlungsbedingung: Durch Überweisung bei Auftragsbestätigung.

Wir sollen Herrn Cullen unseren SWIFT-Code schicken. Die Sendungen werden durch UPS abgeholt, sobald wir Bescheid geben.

G15 (S. 90)

ATMs

Automated teller machines (also **called** instant cash machines in the U.S.) are **computerised** telecommunication devices constructed in **such** a way as to allow **customers** of a bank to make **financial** transactions in a public place **without** having to speak to a cashier or **bank** clerk. Customers simply **insert** their plastic ATM **card**, which has a magnetic strip, or smart card, which has a chip, into the machine. Then the PIN (personal identification **number**) needs to be entered.
If the card is **accepted** by the ATM, a customer can

a) **check** his or her bank **account** balance
b) withdraw **cash** from his or her bank account
c) pre-pay mobile **phone** credit.

ATMs are usually located inside or outside bank **buildings**, in shopping **centres**, or in petrol stations.
Most ATMs are connected to interbank networks so that **people** can also use their cards to **withdraw** money from machines that do not **belong** to their bank.

words that do not appear in the text: overdraw, phone, really

UNIT 6
ORGANIZING TRANSPORT

Content and skills at a glance:

- types of shipments
- writing advices of dispatch
- packaging materials
- caution marks
- means of transport
- review of passive vs. active voice
- logistics

Einleitung

Diese Unit beschäftigt sich mit dem Transport. Wenn ein Auftrag erteilt und die Auftragsbestätigung erfolgt ist, kann der Lieferant die Ware herstellen oder versenden.

Fertiggestellte Ware muss sorgfältig verpackt und, unter Berücksichtigung des vereinbarten Incoterms, versandt werden. Absatz A spricht besonders schwierige Transporte an.

In B geht es um die Versandanzeige oder das Versandavis *(advice of dispatch)*, anhand dessen man dem Kunden mitteilen kann, dass die Ware abholbereit ist bzw. abgeschickt wurde.

Abschnitt C beschäftigt sich mit der Verpackung, Hinweisen zur Handhabung der Ware und der Beibringung der vom Kunden verlangten Dokumente. Wichtig ist, dass die Dokumente die Ware begleiten müssen, um den Export zu ermöglichen. Häufig werden dabei die Dienste eines Spediteurs in Anspruch genommen.

Die Versanddokumente werden erläutert, um dem Lernenden ihre Zuordnung zu ermöglichen. Eine exakte Beschreibung der Tätigkeit eines Spediteurs ist nicht Gegenstand dieser Unit. Der Sprachergänzungstest unter G16 gibt jedoch einen Einblick in das Thema Logistik (als Gesamtbegriff für das Transportwesen), um den Lernenden die Wichtigkeit dieses Geschäftsbereichs zu vermitteln.

Die Kopiervorlage für den **Progress Check** finden Sie auf **S. 91** in diesem Buch.

LÖSUNGEN

A1 (S. 94)

b. flammable; c. perishable; d. explosive; e. toxic; f. valuable; g. refrigeration required; h. heavy and outsized

A2 (S. 95)

students' individual answers

B3 (S. 95)

a. corrugated cardboard, foam rubber; b. the weight and dimensions, the order number and the customer's address; c. Mr. Laskaridis wrote that in his order.; d. From 22 February to 12 March (18 days); e. He has to pay at the latest two weeks after he gets the tea sets.

B4 (S. 96)

a. 2; b. 5; c. 3; d. 6; e. 4; f. 1

C5 (S. 97)

wooden case / wooden box	**Holzkiste**
crate	Lattenkiste
cardboard box	**Pappkarton**
drum	**Trommel**
barrel	Fass
corrugated cardboard	**Wellpappe**
wrapping paper	Packpapier
cushioning material	Füllmaterial
foam rubber	Schaumstoff
heatproof/heat-resistant	**hitzebeständig**
biodegradable	**biologisch abbaubar**
seaworthy	seemäßig

C6 (S. 97)

a. weight and dimensions; b. port of shipment; c. place of destination; d. number of packages; e. order number; f. consignee's marks; g. mark of origin

C7 (S. 99)

a. Packliste; b. Handelsrechnung; c. Pro-forma-Rechnung; d. Ursprungszeugnis; e. Versicherungszertifikat; f. Import-/Exportlizenz

D8 (S. 101)

b. Your order will be sent by UPS on Tuesday, 9 May.
c. Your consignment of office furniture was dispatched yesterday.
d. The television sets can be collected anytime after tomorrow.
e. Each crystal vase has been carefully wrapped according to your instructions.
f. The shipment is expected to reach Dublin on Monday.
g. Payment must be received before your order can be shipped.
h. The consignment has been handed over to your freight forwarders today.
i. Your written order and the packaging instructions have been misplaced by someone in the sales department.
j. Your invoice has not been paid yet.

E9 (S. 102) CD 1 14

questions: a. Julia Perkins is calling Gabi Kellner.; b. Julia Perkins works for Toy World in London. Gabi Kellner works for Spiel und Sport in Augsburg.
words: c. arrange; d. subsidiary; e. tomorrow; f. helpful; g. individually; h. colourful; i. cushioning; j. rough; k. empty; l. fit; m. dispatch; n. pleasure; *extra word:* late

E10 (S. 103)

individual student performances

F11 (S. 105)

Dear Ms Lemon

Advice of dispatch – your order no. 2875

We are pleased to inform you that yesterday we handed over the headphones, model ClearSound 340x, which you ordered on 28 January, to our freight forwarder. The shipment is expected to reach you on 5 February.

As you instructed, we packed the headphones with the utmost care in sturdy cartons with sufficient cushioning material. The required shipping documents (packing list, waybill, commercial invoice, insurance certificate) are enclosed with the shipment.

We trust that the goods will arrive punctually and in good condition and look forward to doing business with you again.

Yours sincerely

AudioStar GmbH

Severin Gassner
Customer Support

F12 (S. 106)

Email

From: ihr.name@granderath-kg.de
To: fred.lange@luminex.com
Sent: May 6, 201_ (or today's date)
Re: Advice of dispatch - your order no. 821-84-x

Dear Mr. Lange,

I am writing to let you know that the consignment of auto lamps as per your order no. 821-84-x is ready to be shipped and will be handed over to the freight forwarder tomorrow. The goods will be taken to Hamburg by rail and then shipped to New York as sea freight on board the MS Albatros. From there the goods will be brought to Cleveland by truck.

The shipment is expected to reach you in four weeks at the latest. As you requested, the auto lights have been packed carefully, and the cases have been marked "Fragile" and "This side up". The shipping documents (a complete set of clean, on-board bills of lading, packing list, commercial invoice, insurance certificate, certificate of origin) will be released by the Bavaria Bank as soon as you accept our 30-day sight draft.

Please let us know as soon as the shipment arrives in Cleveland. We trust that the consignment will reach you in good condition and look forward to the pleasure of serving you again.

Best regards,

(Your Name)
Export Department

G13 (S. 107)

Für:	Herrn Neumann
Verfasst von:	*(Ihr Name)* **am:** ....
E-Mail von:	Frau Katie Winston, Einkaufsabteilung, Toy World Inc., 12321 South Grand Ave., Los Angeles, CA 90015
Datiert:	2. April 201..
Betr.:	Versandanweisungen für Auftrag Nr. 4390 kvt über 72,957.00 €

Frau Winston weist darauf hin, dass alle Kisten mit dem obigen Firmennamen und der Adresse markiert werden müssen. Die Sendung muss außerdem begleitet werden von: einer Pro-forma-Rechnung, dem reinen Konnossement, einem Ursprungszeugnis und einer genauen Packliste.

Wir sollen darauf achten, dass alle Spielwaren dem amerikanischen „Child Protection and Toy Safety Act" (US-Gesetz zum Schutz und zur Sicherheit von Kinderspielzeug) entsprechen müssen.

Außerdem möchte Frau Winston ein Versandavis und eine Kopie der Pro-forma-Rechnung im Voraus erhalten, damit die entsprechenden Vorkehrungen vor Ort getroffen werden können. Sie benötigt auch den Namen des Schiffes und sein Ankunftsdatum in den U.S.A.

G14 (S. 108)

Email

From: peterneumann@spielundsport.de
To: katiewinston@toyworld.com
Sent: 4 April 201_
Re: Your order no. 4390 kvt for toys

Dear Ms. Winston,

Thank you for your e-mail and for the detailed instructions you sent regarding your order no. 4390 kvt. As you requested, all of the cases will be marked with your company's Los Angeles address. Also, we will make sure that the required shipping documents (pro forma invoice, clean bill of lading, certificate of origin, exact packing list) accompany the shipment and will send you copies of all of the documents. A copy of the pro forma invoice will be sent along with the advice of dispatch. As soon as we know the name of the vessel and its arrival date in Los Angeles, we will pass that information on to you.

»

»

For your information, the toys bear the European seal of quality and conform to the requirements of the Child Protection and Toy Safety Act, as required by the US import authorities.

We will be in touch as soon as more information is available. We appreciate your confidence in our company's products and will do everything we can to make sure that this order is handled to your complete satisfaction.

Best regards,

Peter Neumann
Sales Manager

G15 (S. 108) CD 1 15

Für:	Herrn Hans Jürgen Schneider	
Verfasst von:	Anna-Lena Fleischer	**am:** ....
Gesprächspartner/in:	John Gwynn, Eagle Eye Equipment Ltd, Cardiff, GB	
Betr.:	Auftrags-Nr. 74693 vom 14. März für optische Messinstrumente	

Herr Gwynn teilt uns mit, dass sie Probleme mit einem ihrer Lieferanten haben und einige der für die Fertigung benötigten Teile erst Ende der Woche bekommen. Die Lieferung, die morgen fällig wäre, wird sich daher um eine Woche verzögern.

Die einzige Möglichkeit, die Sendung schneller zu bekommen, wäre, sie per Luftfracht zu schicken, aber das ist natürlich viel teurer.

Ich habe Herrn Gwynn gesagt, dass Sie ihn so bald wie möglich anrufen werden. Seine Tel.Nr. ist: 0044 29 2049 7723 oder auf Handy: 0044 7082 455 3682.

G16 (S. 109)

1. commonly; 2. getting; 3. to; 4. at; 5. Every; 6. needs; 7. of; 8. their; 9. efficiently; 10. movement; 11. are made; 12. complicated; 13. more; 14. to; 15. least; 16. warehousing; 17. sometimes; 18. to include; 19. as well; 20. being used; 21. was becoming; 22. field; 23. by; 24. this; 25. precisely; 26. needed; 27. result; 28. which; 29. Like; 30. based

UNIT 7
REQUESTING PAYMENT

Content and skills at a glance:

- writing payment reminders
- invoices and statements of account
- discussing problems with payment
- collection agencies

Einleitung

Das wichtigste Thema im kaufmännischen Bereich ist die Zahlung.
Diese Unit beginnt mit Beispielen der Verfahrensweisen bei verspäteter oder nicht erfolgter Zahlung. Heutzutage werden kaum noch drei, sondern meistens nur noch zwei Mahnungen versandt, bevor gerichtliche Schritte eingeleitet werden oder man ein Inkassoinstitut mit der Zahlungseintreibung beauftragt.
Wichtig ist, die Lernenden auf die förmlichen Unterschiede hinzuweisen. Bei einer ersten Mahnung ist der Ton in der Regel noch höflich und verbindlich; bei einer weiteren Mahnung muss schon etwas schärfer formuliert werden, um unmissverständlich zu verdeutlichen, dass man zu keinen weiteren Konzessionen bereit ist. Ein Beispiel dafür, wie eine solche Situation möglicherweise mündlich geregelt werden kann, hören Sie in dem Telefongespräch in Teil E.

Absatz C beschäftigt sich ausführlich mit der Handelsrechnung *(commercial invoice)*. Basierend auf dem Fall eines Spielzeugverkaufs von Deutschland nach Großbritannien mit einer Zusatzlieferung in die U.S.A. befinden sich unter C 8,9 eine Handelsrechnung mit allen erforderlichen Einzelheiten sowie die entsprechende Proforma-Rechnung an die britische Tochtergesellschaft. Die unterschiedlichen Preise entstehen durch die Wahl der jeweiligen Incoterms. Da die britische Muttergesellschaft beide Rechnungen begleicht, sind die Zahlungsbedingungen identisch: 50 % bei Erhalt der Auftragsbestätigung und 50 % bei Erhalt der Waren in London bzw. Los Angeles, Kalifornien.

Die vier Rechnungstypen (die Handelsrechnung, die Proforma-Rechnung, die Konsulatsrechnung und die Zollrechnung) sollten bereits auf diesem Sprachniveau erlernt werden, da sie im Export von großer Bedeutung sind. Sie werden unter C auf Seite 118 im Lehrbuch im Einzelnen erklärt. Bei Stammkunden ist eine Rechnung nicht unbedingt erforderlich; die Zahlung kann auch auf der Basis eines beiderseitig gehaltenen Kontoauszugs erfolgen (siehe Lehrbuch Seite 122). Hierbei haben sowohl der Verkäufer als auch der Käufer ein Konto des Kunden bzw. Lieferanten, welches sie, je nach vertraglicher Vereinbarung der Zahlungsweise, monatlich, vierteljährlich oder halbjährlich ausgleichen. Dies ist wesentlich einfacher und erspart zusätzliche Papierarbeit. Eventuell entstehende Unstimmigkeiten können mittels Gut- oder Lastschriften ausgeglichen werden.

Die Kopiervorlage für den **Progress Check** finden Sie auf **S. 92** in diesem Buch.

LÖSUNGEN

A1 (S. 112)

possible answers:

a. The customer might
   - not have enough money / be waiting for their own customers to pay / have misplaced the invoice / forgotten to pay / not have paid because there was a mistake on the invoice / not be satisfied with the goods / always wait as long as possible before paying any invoice

b. The customer should immediately inform the supplier and ask for a new corrected invoice.

c. The customer should contact the supplier, tell them about the problem, and make suitable arrangements, perhaps to pay in installments or at a later date.

d. The supplier can send reminders, get a solicitor or collection agency involved, require payment in advance for future orders, or stop doing business with the customer.

B2 (S. 113)

a. T; b. F (The scarves and gloves were shipped this morning and are now on their way.); c. F (The invoice is being sent as an enclosure with the letter.); d. T; e. T

B3 (S. 114)

a. overdue; b. reliable; c. assume; d. misplaced; e. without delay; f. disregard

B4 (S. 115)

possible answers:

a. Payment should have been made by 15 August. *(For this answer, students must refer to the letter on page 113.)*

b. She explains that her company also has to cover its costs, and in order to pay their own bills they need payment from their customers.

c. She asks the customer to let her know about the situation and says they will try to work out a solution together.

d. Sabine sets a deadline of seven days. The customer must either get in touch or pay within that time.

e. Sabine's company will get their solicitors involved and start to take legal action.

B5 (S. 116)

d, c, a, b

B6 (S. 116)

a. of; b. of; c. of; d. in; e. on; f. with; g. in; h. on; i. on

B7 (S. 117)

a. He thanks Ms King for reminding them of the invoice.
b. He apologizes for not contacting Ms King before now.
c. One of Möbel Stern's customers cannot pay Möbel Stern because they have filed bankruptcy. As a result, Möbel Stern does not have enough money to pay their own invoices.
d. Daniel asks for four more weeks in which to pay.
e. His second suggestion is to pay half of the amount within one week and the other half six weeks later.
f. He asks her to get in touch and let him know if she can agree to one of the suggestions.
g. He hopes that the two companies will still be able to do business together despite this delay in payment.

C8 (S. 119)

a. The country of origin is Germany.; b. The toys are being shipped to Toy World Ltd, 64 Queen Victoria Street, London EC4V 4JA, UK.; c. The shipment will weigh 2,800 kg.; d. The toys will be shipped on pallets.; e. The invoice was written in Augsburg.

C9 (S. 120)

The only formal difference is the heading. Otherwise a pro forma invoice includes the same information as a commercial invoice. In this particular case, the company in Los Angeles is receiving a pro forma invoice they do not have to pay; payment will be made by the company headquarters in Britain. The company in Britain is receiving a commercial invoice because they have to pay for the goods being sent to them.

C10 (S. 121)

a. pleased; b. collect; c. advised; d. includes; e. agreed; f. respectively; g. appreciate; h. initial

C11 (S. 122)

a. regular; b. lists; c. received; d. advantages; e. process; f. adds; g. agreed

D12 (S. 123)

a. remit, settle, transfer; b. outstanding, overdue; c. amount, balance, sum, total; d. debit, deduct, subtract; *The word "credit" does not fit in any of the categories.*

D13 (S. 123)

a. We are writing to let you know that our invoice no. 83641 dated 21 April has not been paid yet.
b. We would ask that you remit the amount due to our account within two weeks.
c. We assume that this is an oversight. / We assume that the invoice has been misplaced or forgotten.
d. We must insist that the overdue amount be transferred to our account immediately.
e. Please accept our apologies for not yet having paid your invoice no. 83641 dated 21 April.
f. Could we pay in monthly instalments of €450?
g. Thank you very much for your understanding and patience.

E14 (S. 123) CD 1 16

Quantity	Product	Article No.	Unit Price	Total Price
50	Wooden pyramids	682-L	€50.00	€2,500.00
25	Nutcrackers	449-K	€25.00	€ 625.00

E15 (S. 124) CD 1 16

a. She wanted to point out a problem with an invoice and get it corrected.
b. She should throw it away as soon as she gets the new invoice.
c. They got a new computer system installed recently and had to enter some data by hand during the transition period.
d. Christmas is the peak season for wooden pyramids and nutcrackers.
e. Twice. He says, "I do apologize for the inconvenience" and "Please accept our apologies once again".

E16 (S. 124)

individual student performances

F17 (S. 125)

Email

Re: Your email about our statement of account no. 32098

Dear Elmar,

Thanks for your email and for letting me know about the problem with your statement of account. I'm really sorry that we forgot to include the discount. I made a note of it after our phone conversation, but then obviously forgot to change the statement. It won't happen again, I promise!

»

»

I'll make the correction right away and send you the corrected statement as soon as possible. Once again, I apologize for the mistake and assure you that it won't happen again. Have a good day!

Best regards,

Jennifer

G18 (S. 126)

Freytag AG
Zugspitzstr. 29-31
82481 Mittenwald

31 May 201_

Mr Angus McGregor
Machine Tools Limited
56 Lomond Avenue
Glasgow G43 5FD
Großbritanien

Dear Mr McGregor

Second and final reminder: last instalment

Two months ago we delivered a machine tool, type GF 420, to your company. Payment was to be made in three instalments of €11,000.00 each. The first instalment arrived punctually. The second instalment arrived with a delay of three weeks. We are now writing to remind you that the final instalment of €11,000.00 is one month overdue. Unfortunately we have not received a response to the reminder we sent two weeks ago.

We must insist that the outstanding amount be transferred to our account immediately. You will certainly understand that we need to meet our own financial obligations. If there are any special circumstances preventing you from making payment, please let us know. Perhaps we can make arrangements to grant you a payment deferral.

»

››

Should we not hear from you or receive payment within two weeks from today, we will have no alternative but to place the matter in the hands of our solicitors. We hope that this situation can be resolved amicably and hope to hear from you in the very near future.

Yours sincerely
Freytag AG

Wilhelm Städter
Export Manager

G19 (S. 127)

Dear Mr Evans

Your *outstanding* balance of €4,500.00

Strickwaren Bergland GmbH **have** entrusted us with the **collection** of the overdue amount of €2,140.00, which was **due** at the end of August and has not yet been **remitted**.

The final **deadline** has elapsed without the company **being** credited with the outstanding **sum**.

They have therefore **placed** the matter in our hands, and we must **inform** you that we will file an action **against** you at the local **court** in Frankfurt.

Should you wish to **avoid** any inconvenience and further **costs**, you still have the opportunity to **transfer** the sum to our **account** (see below) or to the account of Strickwaren Bergland GmbH. If not, you will **receive** further instructions from our **solicitors** and the Frankfurt Court.

Yours **sincerely**
Brand & Hörbiger

Daniela Frey
Collection **Agent**

(*words that do not appear in the text:* bank, debtor, reminder)

G20 (S. 128)

Für:	Herrn Hans-Jörg Bamberger, Geschäftsführer	
Verfasst von:	*(Ihr Name)*	**am:** ....
Brief von:	Uns als Antwort auf Mahnung von Frau King	
Unterzeichner:	Daniel Ganter	
Betr.:	Mahnung wegen der ausstehenden Rechnung von Frau King Nr. 97-43-145 über 10.160,00 €	

Wir haben heute die obige Mahnung für die Rechnung, die Ende August fällig war, beantwortet. Herr Ganter hat sich dafür entschuldigt, dass wir nicht eher geantwortet haben und als Begründung für die Verspätung angegeben, dass einer unserer Hauptkunden Insolvenz angemeldet hat. Herr Ganter hat geschrieben, dass wir aus diesem Grund unverschuldet gewisse finanzielle Schwierigkeiten haben und einen Zahlungsaufschub von vier Wochen erbitten. Als Alternative hat er angeboten, dass wir die Hälfte des Rechnungsbetrages innerhalb einer Woche und den Rest sechs Wochen später begleichen.

Wir warten jetzt auf Antwort.

UNIT 8
REDUCING RISKS

Content and skills at a glance:

- insurance
- making credit enquiries in writing and on the phone
- transport accidents
- false friends
- Lloyd's of London

Einleitung

Diese Unit ist der Reduzierung der Risiken gewidmet, also der Absicherung, dass die bestellte Ware bezahlt wird. Dies geschieht zum einen durch das Einholen von Auskünften und zum anderen durch den Abschluss einer die Risiken abdeckenden Versicherung.

Unter B werden Kreditanfragen und Kreditauskünfte behandelt, anhand derer ein Unternehmen sich versichert, ob der Kunde solvent ist.
Die Übungen dieser Unit befassen sich mit dem Einholen und Geben von Auskünften verschiedener Art.

Absatz C gibt einen Einblick in das Versicherungswesen. Bedingt durch das sprachliche Niveau, kann dieses Thema nur in groben Zügen behandelt werden. Ziel ist es, die Lernenden langsam in die komplexe Thematik einzuführen und Ihnen zu verdeutlichen, wie eine entsprechende Versicherung aussehen sollte.
Eine ausführliche Beschreibung der Versicherung zur Abdeckung von Transportrisiken finden Sie auf Seite 138.

Die Übungen D 10,11 auf Seite 139 behandeln die oft zu wenig beachteten *false friends*, die bei inkorrekter Anwendung im richtigen Geschäftsleben durchaus zu lustigen Verwechslungen führen können. Die Übungen eignen sich gut als Unterrichtseinstieg oder Auflockerung für zwischendurch.

Im Sprachergänzungstest in G 17 wird Lloyd´s of London, der größte Versicherungsmarkt der Welt, vorgestellt. Bei fortgeschrittenen Lernenden kann dieser Text als Übersetzungsübung zum besseren Verständnis dieser schwierigen Materie herangezogen werden. Bei Bedarf können weitere Informationen aus dem Internet den Unterricht beleben.

Die Kopiervorlage für den **Progress Check** finden Sie auf **S. 93** in diesem Buch.

LÖSUNGEN

A1 (S. 131)

a. an insurance policy; b. a premium; c. a claim; d. damages

A2 (S. 131)

Most people have health insurance, life insurance and car insurance. Many also have household insurance. Typical types of insurance that companies have include property insurance, liability insurance and casualty insurance.

B3 (S. 133)

Notes in English:

- Elegy Electronics Ltd is a new customer of ours.
- We'd like information on their finances, reputation and reliability.
- Can we grant credit of £25,000 without risk?
- Any information will be treated confidentially.
- We would be glad to give you similar information if needed.

B4 (S. 134)

a. in question; b. reason for complaint; c. reliable; d. proprietors; e. considerable capital; f. as a result; g. obligation on our part; h. it will be handled with strict confidence

B5 (S. 135)

a. This is a negative credit information letter.
b. The problems began during the past year.
c. The letter mentions late payment and a lack of communication.
d. He thinks that Samuelson, Inc. is having financial problems and ordering more goods than they can afford to pay for.
e. He recommends being careful when selling goods to Samuelson and asking for payment in advance.

B6 (S. 136)

a. We are sorry to tell you that ... / Unfortunately we have to tell you that ...
b. ... we cannot give you ...
c. ... what you asked for / the details you asked for.
d. ... if they say it is all right / if they say it is OK.
e. ... to help you with this situation / to help you in this case.

C7 (S. 137) CD 1 17

a. truck (AE) / lorry (BE); b. train; c. ship

C8 (S. 137)

a. collided; b. capsized; c. derailed

C9 (S. 139)

a. Kitchen Specialists is the buyer.; b. Backmeister GmbH is the seller.; c. The insured property is 10 industrial ovens and 10 industrial mixers. d. The insurer is Loyola Versicherungen.; e. The responsibility for providing insurance will pass from Backmeister GmbH to Kitchen Specialists when the goods have been loaded on board the ship in Bremerhaven.

D10 (S. 139)

Individual student answers could include some of the following:

German	English	English	German
Menü	daily special	menu	Speisekarte
Pension	small hotel	pension	Rente
Rat	advice	rat	Ratte
Chef	boss	chef	Chefkoch
Gift	poison	gift	Geschenk
sensibel	sensitive	sensible	vernünftig
tasten	touch	taste	kosten
etc.			

D11 (S. 139)

a. beamer → digital projector; b. police → policy; c. guilty → valid; d. actual → current; e. caution → deposit; f. prospect → brochure; g. loan → salary; h. fabric → factory

a. The word "beamer" is an American expression for a BMW.
b. The "police" are officials who wear uniforms and make sure that people obey the law.
c. The word "guilty" means responsible for breaking a law.
d. The word "actual" means real.
e. "Caution" is care and attention given in a difficult situation.
f. A "prospect" can be the possibility that something good will happen OR it can mean a possible customer.
g. A "loan" is a sum of money that is borrowed, usually from a bank, and has to be paid back.
h. "Fabric" is another word for cloth or woven material.

D12 (S. 140)

a. mobile phone (BE), cell phone (AE); b. spa; c. exercise bike; d. gym; e. bullying; f. dinner jacket (BE), tuxedo (AE)

E13 (S. 140) CD 1 18

a. Alissa asks about Maschinenbau Huber GmbH.
b. She needs information about them because they are a new client and she wants to find out if they are reliable before doing work for them.

c. Linda does not tell Alissa how much money Maschinenbau Huber spends with them each month.

E14 (S. 140) CD 1 18

a. receptionist; b. credit; c. references; d. campaign; e. reliable; f. strict; g. detail; h. difficulties; i. promptly; j. consider; k. release; l. obligation; *extra word:* policy

E15 (S. 141)

Individual student performances

F16 (S. 143)

Email

Dear Ellen,

I'm writing in response to the email you sent yesterday about Sport Schumann. Unfortunately we are not in a position to give you the information you asked for. Sport Schumann is a new customer of ours, and for this reason we can't judge their creditworthiness or reliability yet.

However, you could contact Sport Langer in Augsburg. As far as I know, they are a long-term customer of Sport Schumann. Their email address is info@sportartikel_langer.eu.

I'm sorry that I wasn't able to help. If you need similar information in the future, just let me know, and if we have experience dealing with the customer, I'll be happy to tell you what you need to know.

Best regards,

(Your name)

G17 (S. 144)

Lloyd's of London

Insurance **can** be taken out from an insurance company or from Lloyd's of London, which is the **most** famous insurance market in the **world**.

The market **began** over 300 years ago in Edward Lloyd's coffeehouse in Tower Street, London. This coffeehouse was a **popular** place for merchants and ship owners **to meet** and discuss the latest shipping news. These discussions led to arrangements **between** the shipping industry and people who **were** prepared to insure shipping risks.

After several fundamental changes in the **structure** of Lloyd's and many problems **arising** from the full liability which Lloyd's insurers **had to** accept **until then**, the Second Lloyd's

Act was **passed** in 1982. This act redefined the management structure and set rules **for** the British insurance market **which** Lloyd's of London operates.

The **policies** written at Lloyd's are backed by members, **referred** to as Names. About 10% of these Names are individuals, **while** the remaining 90% are companies with **limited** liability. The members are **grouped** into syndicates.

Lloyd's brokers act as **intermediaries** between the clients who buy insurance and the underwriters who sell it. Negotiations between brokers and underwriters take place in the Room of Lloyd's, which in some ways functions like a street market. On **behalf** of their clients, the brokers negotiate insurance **premiums** with the underwriters **until** they have obtained full insurance cover for the product or service **their** clients wish to **insure.** Only **then** is the Lloyd's policy issued. Since Lloyd's of London is a very large insurance market with a **high** turnover, Lloyd's policies are nearly **always** backed by several underwriters **from** various syndicates.

G18 (S. 145)

Email

From: ingrid.thanning@laehrl.eu
To: nicholas.flynn@automotiveexperts.co.uk
Sent: 14 January 201_
Re.: Your credit enquiry

Dear Mr Flynn

In response to your credit enquiry, I am pleased to report that Stiedl & Söhne is a reliable customer of ours and has placed orders with us regularly for several years. Payment is usually made punctually. Our terms of payment with them are 30 days net.

Stiedl & Söhne is a solid family-run business. The eldest son took over management of the company a year ago. We would have no reservations about granting a line of credit in the amount you mentioned.

This information is given without any obligation on our part, and we trust that it will be handled confidentially. Please feel free to contact me again if you need further information.

Yours sincerely

Ingrid Thanning
Finance Director

G19 (S. 146)

Für:	Frau Marianne Fichtner
Verfasst von:	*(Ihr Name)* **am: ....**
Betr.:	Brief von Dan Mathers, Accounting Manager, vom … bezüglich unserer Bitte um Auskunft über die Firma Samuelson, Inc.

Herr Mathers teilt uns mit, dass die Erfahrungen seines Unternehmens mit Samuelson, Inc. nicht immer zufriedenstellend ausfielen. Sie waren zwar seit 2005 mehrere Jahre gute und zuverlässige Kunden, fingen während des letzten Jahres jedoch an, nicht mehr pünktlich zu zahlen und sprachen auch nicht offen über ihre Probleme. Sie mussten mehrmals angemahnt werden, es wurde sogar mit Klage gedroht.

Offensichtlich hat das Unternehmen finanzielle Schwierigkeiten und scheint sich diesbezüglich zu übernehmen.

Herr Mathers empfiehlt, Aufträge dieses Unternehmens nur mit Vorauskasse anzunehmen. Er weist darauf hin, dass seine Auskunft unverbindlich ist und von uns streng vertraulich behandelt werden muss.

UNIT 9
HANDLING COMPLAINTS

Content and skills at a glance:

- making complaints
- responding to complaints
- production sectors
- describing damaged goods

Einleitung

Ein leidiges Thema jeglicher Handelskorrespondenz sind Beschwerden aller Art. Diesen eine ganze Unterrichtseinheit zu widmen ist jedoch sinnvoll, da es sich häufig um gute Kunden oder gute Lieferanten handelt, denen man eine Beschwerde melden muss. Dies erfordert ein gewisses Fingerspitzengefühl. Ist die Sachlage klar, gibt es in der Regel kein Problem; oft ist es aber nicht so einfach. Zu klären sind Fragen wie z. B.: Wer ist wirklich schuld? Soll ich mich stur verhalten oder nachgeben? Lohnt es sich, bei einem so guten Kunden einen Aufstand zu machen und Hilfe zu verweigern, nur weil man sich im Recht glaubt?

Hinzu kommen die sprachlichen Unterschiede. Hier hat die Lehrkraft eine gute Gelegenheit darauf hinzuweisen, dass man im Deutschen relativ „krass" ist und Dinge direkt anspricht (z.B. *Sie haben das falsch geliefert!*), während der Engländer oder Amerikaner dies viel höflicher ausdrückt (*I´m afraid to say that you seem to have delivered the wrong goods!*). Bei einer größeren Lerngruppe eignen sich an dieser Stelle entsprechende mündliche Übungen.
In dem Telefongespräch unter E 11 reagiert der Anrufer für britisch/amerikanische Verhältnisse ausnahmsweise sehr unwirsch. Das kommt natürlich vor, wenn jemand verärgert ist, trägt jedoch selten zur Lösung des Problems bei.

Teil C ist den Produktionssektoren gewidmet. Die aus der Volkswirtschaft entlehnten Begriffe sollten auch auf diesem Niveau schon erlernt werden; z.B. um zu verstehen, warum der Handel in den dritten Produktionsbereich gehört. Übung C 7 auf Seite 156 kann in diese Richtung ausgedehnt und beliebig erweitert werden. Eine mögliche Diskussionsanregung wäre die folgende Frage: ‚Warum ist auch ein Sektor, der nichts herstellt, für das Finanzamt wegen des Steueraufkommens wichtig?'
Der Sprachergänzungstest auf Seite 163 beschäftigt sich ebenfalls mit den Produktionssektoren.

Die Kopiervorlage für den **Progress Check** finden Sie auf **S. 94** in diesem Buch.

LÖSUNGEN

A1 (S. 149)
students' individual answers

A2 (S. 150)
possible ideas:

a. They should listen to what the customer says, make sure that they understand the situation, show the customer that they understand the situation, remain calm, get help from a colleague or manager if necessary, and then decide how to handle the complaint.
b. Of course, the customer is not always right. Sometimes customers make mistakes or unreasonable demands. However, the customer should usually be given the feeling that he or she is always right. After all, the customer pays the bills. If a relationship with a customer becomes too unpleasant, a company may decide not to do business with that customer any more.
c. Complaints are good in two main ways: (1) They give a company feedback about what area of their business they need to improve, and (2) they show that customers care enough to try to work out a solution. The worst situation for a company is if dissatisfied customers don't complain but simply take their business somewhere else.

B3 (S. 151)
a. consignment; b. as per; c. obviously; d. noticeable; e. urgently; f. needed; g. plant; h. matter

B4 (S. 152)
a. "Short shipped" means that too few products were sent.
b. Not enough Ferrari red picture frames were delivered; he got 45 instead of 50. Also, a wrong product was delivered (light oak picture frames instead of dark oak picture frames).
c. Justin will keep them until Ms Mueller tells him what to do with them.
d. He asks her to tell him when she has read this e-mail and to let him know when the missing and correct items will be delivered.

B5 (S. 153)
Ronald Schiller of Heinrichs wrote to Jeremy Stones of Machinery Exports as follows:
- He is sorry to hear that contents of case no. 4 were damaged
- Case no. 4 left Heinrichs in perfect condition
- Damage must have occurred in transit
- He has contacted Heinrichs' insurance company
- A full set of new spare parts will be shipped via airmail free of charge
- Arrival at Manchester airport on cargo flight BA 39810 tomorrow at 4.35 p.m.
- Case must be collected by Machinery Exports

B6 (S. 154)

a. 6, b. 2; c. 5; d. 1; e. 3; f. 4

C7 (S. 155)

Primary production: fishing, gold mining, oil drilling
Secondary production: furniture production, pharmaceuticals, plastics
Tertiary production: freight forwarding, health care, legal services, restaurants, wholesalers

C8 (S. 156)

a. end user; b. business-to-business; c. wholesaler; d. retail; e. consumers; f. subsidiary; g. distributor; h. commission; i. possession; j. reselling

D9 (S. 156)

a. stained; b. scratched; c. bent; d. broken; e. cracked; f. dented

D10 (S. 157)

a. The consignment as per our order no. 50018, which should have arrived two weeks ago, has not arrived yet.
b. On examining the shipment that arrived yesterday, we noticed that several items are missing.
c. We would ask you to replace the damaged goods without delay.
d. We are looking into the matter.
e. We assure you that we will do our utmost to resolve this matter in a way which is satisfactory for all of us.
f. Please accept our sincere apologies for any inconvenience caused.

E11 (S. 157) CD 1 19

A shipment of dictionaries is late. Mark Mendelson calls to complain. Rita handles the situation more effectively by remaining calm and being helpful.

E12 (S. 157) CD 1 19

a. He ordered TechnoDict 2020 dictionaries.
b. The shipment was supposed to arrive a week ago.
c. The order number is 746/900.
d. He needs the dictionaries for an important book fair.
e. She puts him on hold and calls UPS to see where the shipment is.

E13 (S. 157)

possible answers:

Listen to the customer. Make sure you understand the situation. Show the customer that you understand their situation. Remain calm. Do not take the customer's anger personally. Get help from a colleague or manager if necessary.

E14 (S. 158)

individual student performances

F15 (S. 159)

Dear Ms Austen

Complaint regarding shipment of jewellery boxes as per our order no. 67671

The jewellery boxes we ordered from you on 10 October arrived on schedule. However, I have to inform you that the goods did not arrive in good condition. At least 75 of the 150 jewellery boxes are damaged and therefore unusable. Apparently the cartons were handled roughly in transit, which led to the damage we found.

For your information, I am enclosing several photos that clearly show the damage. Since we need the jewellery boxes urgently for a trade fair, we would ask you to replace the damaged goods without delay.

We trust that you will deal with this matter quickly and look forward to hearing from you very soon.

Yours sincerely

(Your name)
Purchasing Manager

Encs

G16 (S. 160)

Marine Insurance Ltd
154, Valley Road
Chorley PR 6 5HN
United Kingdom

Mr Peter Norman
GFB Australia Pty. Ltd.
40 North Creek Road
NSW 2099 Dee Why West
Australia

Dear Mr Norman

Delivery of 100 barrels of bitumen / Your insurance policy No. SWKLF 5390, insurance certificate No. 360/2012

We have received notification of your claim along with the documentation you sent. In order to process this claim, we still require the following documents:

- a damage report prepared by an average adjuster
- a copy of the clean marine bill of lading issued by the captain of the Mary Ann the invoice for the replacement barrels of bitumen

After we have examined the documents, the corresponding amount will be transferred to the account of GFB Australia.

Please make sure to carefully examine the barrels and monitor their storage on board the ship in future.

Yours sincerely

Harry Swift
Claims Adjustment Department

G17 (S. 161)

Für:	Herrn Geschäftsführer Johannes Eder	
Verfasst von:	*(Ihr Name)*	**am:** ....
E-Mail von:	Machinery Experts, Manchester, GB	
Unterzeichner:	Jeremy Stones, Einkaufsabteilung	
Betr:	Schadensmeldung - Auftrags-Nr. des Kunden: KLFSU 250 vom 15. Januar 201_ – Dringende Ersatzteillieferung!	

Herr Stones teilt uns mit, dass Kiste Nr. 4 mit den Ersatzteilen für seine Maschine SP 300 während des Transports beschädigt wurde. Obwohl von außen keinerlei Beschädigung festzustellen war, hatte die Kiste innen einen Riss und die Ersatzteile sind zerbrochen und daher unbrauchbar.

Herr Stones hat eine Liste der beschädigten Teilen und ein Foto beigefügt. Er bittet um sofortigen Ersatz, da die Teile dringend benötigt werden.

Da die Lieferung DAP an die Fabrik des Kunden in Manchester erfolgte, müssen wir bei unserer Versicherung den Schaden melden. Herr Stones gab uns im Falle weiterer Nachfragen seine Tel.Nr. an: 0044 39571 0769.

G18 (S. 162)

Production sectors

There are **three** sectors of production. First, there is the primary field, **where** we take, or harvest, the **gifts** nature has provided us with. Then there is manufacturing, where we use some **sort** of secondary production process to improve on nature's raw materials. And **finally** there is the tertiary sector, which includes not only trading – where we **buy** and sell later at a profit – but also services that **require** materials, for **example** the truck a lorry driver buys to **transport** products from one place to another. There are also services **which** do not necessarily use materials, but instead rely on specific **knowledge** to advise or help **people** when setting up businesses or doing their daily work. These services could include insurance or banking. The public sector often provides services to the **general** public at subsidized prices to **ensure** that every member of society can make **use** of them. Examples are **schools**, hospitals, parks and public gardens, leisure facilities **like** swimming pools or sporting **areas**, the supply of gas and electricity for the **households**, and building and maintaining **roads** and motorways, among others.

words that do not appear in the text: but, never, temporary

UNIT 10
TRAVELLING FOR BUSINESS

Content and skills at a glance:

- hotel services and amenities
- making travel arrangements
- some types of companies in the US and UK
- meetings

Einleitung

Diese Unit widmet sich der Organisation und Buchung von Geschäftsreisen.

Abschnitt C macht die Lernenden mit verschiedenen Rechtsformen von Gesellschaften vertraut. Natürlich kann das Thema auf diesem Sprachniveau nicht im Detail vertieft werden; vielmehr ist es eine erste Einführung in die in GB und den USA gängigen Abkürzungen der Gesellschaften und eine Erläuterung dieser Gesellschaftsformen. Beides ist erforderlich, um Adressen von Firmen richtig verstehen und schreiben zu können, und um zu interpretieren, um welche Art von Gesellschaft es sich handelt.

Die Lernenden sollten auf die Unterschiede zwischen Personen- und Kapitalgesellschaften hingewiesen werden, da dies bei der Durchführung von Geschäften bezüglich der Solvenz und Haftung durchaus wichtig sein kann. Ebenfalls zu beachten sind die unterschiedlichen Unternehmensformen und deren Bezeichnungen in GB und den USA.

Im Sprachergänzungstest auf Seite 180 im Lehrbuch werden Vokabeln und Einzelheiten von Meetings angesprochen, die bei fast allen Konferenz- oder Tagungsreisen auf dem Programm stehen.

Die Kopiervorlage für den **Progress Check** finden Sie auf **S. 95** in diesem Buch.

LÖSUNGEN

A1 (S. 167)
b. air conditioning; c. airport shuttle; d. car park; e. comfortable beds; f. continental breakfast; g. convenient location; h. fitness room; i. high-speed internet access; j. widescreen TV

A2 (S. 167)
students' individual answers

B3 (S. 168)
a. return; b. direct; c. aisle; d. near; e. access; f. advance

B4 (S. 169)
a. for; b. from; c. to; d. for; e. from; f. at; g. on; h. at; i. in; j. at; k. on; l. from; m. at; n. on; o. at; p. at; q. on; r. at; s. for; t. from

B5 (S. 169)
a. cheapest, least expensive; b. the money for the ticket cannot be returned; c. costing a lot more money; d. things that make a stay more pleasant for guests; e. a less expensive room price

B6 (S. 170)
suggested answers:
It may not be necessary for businesspeople to fly business class
- on short flights / if the company needs to save money / if it is certain that the flight dates won't have to be changed / if the businessperson has time to recover before his or her business meeting.

It may make sense to pay more for a business-class ticket
- for long flights / if the businessperson needs to go to a meeting right after arriving / if the businessperson needs to do some work on the flight / if the date of the return flight is uncertain and may need to be changed.

C7 (S. 170)
a. limited liability partnership; b. limited (Ltd also stands for "private limited company".); c. corporation; d. managing director; e. chief executive officer; f. incorporated; g. public limited company; *extra expression:* incorporation

C8 (S. 170)
a. capital; b. profit; c. debt; d. creditors; e. liable; f. limited

C9 (S. 172)

a. F (In a general partnership, the partners are liable for losses and debts with their business and private capital.)
b. T
c. T
d. T
e. F (The abbreviation 'Inc.' can be used for privately held or publicly traded companies in the US.)
f. T (dividends - NB: Im Deutschen werden hierfür unterschiedliche Begriffe verwendet. Eine *Dividende* wird von einer Aktiengesellschaft an ihre Aktionäre ausbezahlt. Bei einer GmbH spricht man stattdessen von einer *Gewinnausschüttung*.)
g. F (In a publicly traded company, a general meeting of shareholders generally takes place once a year.)
h. F (Only the executive members of the board of directors manage the daily activities of a publicly traded company.)

C10 (S. 173)

possible answers:

b. I'd like to introduce Terence J. Williams. He is the Chief Executive Officer, or CEO, of an American stock corporation called Bridgetown Corporation. In Britain this would correspond to the Chairman of the Board of the PLC.
c. This is Luisa Marin Suárez. She works for Harrison & Partners LLP in Swansea, Wales. An LLP is a limited liability partnership. Luisa works as a coordinator in the purchasing department.
d. I'd like you to meet Gabriele Slowinsky. She is the managing director of a German "GmbH" company. This is similar to a private limited company, or Ltd, in Britain.

D11 (S. 174)

a. boarding pass / passport; b. duty free / free parking; c. fitness room / room service; d. stopover / overbooked; e. carry-on luggage / luggage storage service; f. full English breakfast / breakfast buffet

D12 (S. 174)

Hotel vocabulary: free parking, fitness room, room service, overbooked, luggage storage service, full English breakfast, breakfast buffet
Air travel vocabulary: duty free, stopover, overbooked, carry-on luggage

D13 (S. 174)

a. *personal* should be *personnel*; b. *convenient* should be *comfortable*; c. *travel* should be *trip*; d. *comfortable* should be *convenient*; e. *require* should be *request*

D14 (S. 175)

a. reasonable prices; b. favourable terms of payment; c. a convenient location; d. favourable references; e. convenient to reach; f. a comfortable chair; g. convenient operation; h. a lazy person; i. comfortable shoes

E15 (S. 175) CD 1 20

a. Maple Leaf Air; b. 13 April; c. 18 April; d. Garden Courtyard Hotel

E16 (S. 175) CD 1 20

a. F (Ms Eberhard booked an aisle seat in economy class.); b. F (Her seat assignment is 22D.); c. T; d. T; e. F (The hotel room costs 189 Canadian dollars.); f. T; g. F (Ms Eberhard's first name is Lesley.); h. T

E17 (S. 176)

individual student performances

F18 (S. 177)

Dear Ann

I'm writing to give you some information about Markus Simon's upcoming trip to Singapore. He'll be departing from Frankfurt on flight no. LH 790, leaving at 9:40 p.m. on 2 September and arriving in Singapore at 3:55 p.m. on 3 September.

Could you arrange to pick him up at the airport? He'll be staying at the Golden Palm Hotel.

Mr Simon would like to invite the entire staff to dinner on 5 September. Could you reserve a table at a suitable restaurant?

For your information, Mr Simon's return flight, no. LH 788, leaves Singapore at 11:05 p.m. on 6 September. He's looking forward to seeing Mr Lee and having a productive stay in Singapore.

Have a good day!

Best regards

(Ihr Name)

F19 (S. 178)

The Deininger Family is pleased to welcome you to their family-run hotel and hopes you have a pleasant stay.

Comfortable single, double or triple rooms are designed to make your stay as restful as possible. All of the rooms in our hotel are non-smoking rooms and equipped with colour television, radio and WiFi as well as en suite facilities.

Because of our hotel's convenient location, you can reach the New Munich Trade Fair Centre in approx. 10 minutes, Munich Airport in approx. 20 minutes and the Munich city centre in aprox. 30 minutes.

G20 (S. 179) CD 1 21

Für: Herrn Karl Neuhaus
Verfasst von: Tanja Buchner **am:** ....
Gesprächspartner/in: Sam Wellington, Empire Hotel, Sydney, Australien
Betr.: Hotelreservierung für die Messe im März in Sydney

Ich habe heute das Empire Hotel in Sydney angerufen und vom 3. bis 8. März zwei Einzelzimmer für Janine Forster und Markus Merkel reserviert. Da die Zimmer mit Blick auf den Hafen 169 A$ pro Nacht kosten und ich das etwas teuer fand, habe ich die Zimmer ohne Hafenblick für 129 A$ pro Nacht genommen.

Des Weiteren habe ich ein Doppelzimmer vom 3. bis 10. März für Sie und Ihre Frau bestellt. Da Sie Ihren 25. Hochzeitstag feiern, dachte ich, Sie möchten ein Zimmer mit Hafenblick haben, das kostet aber 249 A$ pro Nacht. Ich habe das vorsorglich reserviert, aber das Hotel hält uns die Option für ein billigeres Zimmer offen. Wir müssen uns jedoch wegen der Messe schnell entscheiden.

Die Zimmerpreise schließen ein Frühstücksbuffet von 7 bis 10 Uhr morgens ein. Alle Zimmer sind Nichtraucher-Zimmer und haben ein Bad mit Dusche. Nur die Suiten haben eine Dusche und eine Wanne. Sie sind außerdem alle mit WLAN und einem Flachbild-Fernseher mit Pay-TV ausgerüstet. Garagenplätze in der Hotelgarage kosten 15 A$ pro Tag. Ich habe einen Platz vom 03.03.–10.03. gebucht. Es gibt einen Shuttle-Service vom und zum Flughafen.

Falls Ihre Frau Hilfe bei der Programmgestaltung braucht, kann ihr der Concierge jederzeit behilflich sein.

G21 (S. 179)

Email

From: info@alpenhotelhuber.de
To: jennifer.simpson@UKmail.co.uk
Subject: Your enquiry about rooms from 15th to 30th July

Dear Ms Simpson

Thank you for your interest in our hotel. We have two double rooms available for the time period you requested, and all of the rooms in our hotel are non-smoking. A double room in the main building with a balcony and a view of the mountains costs €110 per night. For rooms without a balcony, the cost is €95. You may also be interested in a suite for up to five people, which costs €140 per night and is ideal for families.

An extensive breakfast buffet is included in the price. Guests are also welcome to use our nice outdoor swimming pool. For your information, I am attaching an information sheet listing leisure time activities in Ruhpolding as well as a booking (reservation) form stating our terms of payment.

Please feel free to contact us at any time if you need further information. We would recommend that you make your reservation soon since a lot of people in Germany are on holiday at the end of July. We look forward to hearing from you soon.

Best regards

Franz Huber
Hotel Manager

G22 (S. 180)

Meetings

In business meetings, people come **together** to share information, make **decisions** and negotiate deals. Traditionally, people had to attend meetings in person, often requiring them to take long and expensive **business trips.** Thanks to developments in communication **technology**, conference calls using the telephone and video conferences using software such as Skype have become an integral part of business life, particularly for **companies** that do business internationally.

Although telephone and video conferencing have become **increasingly** common, sometimes a face-to-face meeting is the most effective way to build business **relationships** and reach agreement on complex issues. In order to be **effective**, a meeting must be **carefully planned**. An agenda outlines the structure of the meeting and lists the points to be **discussed**. To keep a record of the meeting, someone will be asked to take the minutes. This written **summary** of what was discussed and decided during the meeting should be sent to all of the **participants** as soon as possible after the meeting is over. Ideally, the minutes should include an **action plan** to remind everyone specifically what needs to be done to follow up on the meeting.

Sales meetings between customers and **suppliers** are common and can be arranged as needed. **Trade fairs** are an ideal venue for suppliers to meet as many **customers** as possible within a short period of **time**. Staff meetings, team meetings and project meetings **facilitate** communication among employees and help to organize the workflow. Regularly scheduled **board meetings** and annual shareholder meetings allow upper **management** to present results and make decisions that will affect the future of the company.

words that do not appear in the text: however, terminology, underground

UNIT 11

EXHIBITING AT TRADE FAIRS

Content and skills at a glance:

- trade fair vocabulary
- organizing trade fair participation
- advertising
- word forms
- disagreeing politely
- the advertising agency

Einleitung

Unit 11 beschäftigt sich mit Fachmessen.
Sie behandelt die Teilnahme an Messen, die Ausstattung eines Messestandes sowie das dafür relevante Vokabular. Das Telefonat unter E 15 liefert ein Beispiel für die mündliche Buchung und Organisation eines Messeauftritts und wird als „Vermerk über ein Gespräch" unter G 20 auf Seite 196 im Lehrbuch wieder aufgegriffen.

Wichtig in diesem Zusammenhang ist das weit gefasste Gebiet der Werbung, welches in Unit 2 unter dem Oberbegriff Marketing schon ansatzweise angesprochen wurde. Die Werbung als Teilbereich des Marketings beschäftigt sich mit der Vermarktung des Produkts oder der Dienstleistung. Die theoretische Einleitung in diesen Bereich erfolgt unter C 7, 8 auf den Seiten 190–191 im Lehrbuch, gefolgt von einer praktischen Übung unter C 9 auf Seite 191.

Die Sprachübungen unter D geben den Lernenden die Möglichkeit, Wörter zu bilden und dadurch ihren Wortschatz zu erweitern. Diese Übungsart kann mit einer Vielzahl anderer Wörter (*sell, buy, examine, inspect,* usw.) durchgeführt werden. Unter E wird dargestellt, wie man diplomatisch eine abweichende Meinung ausdrücken kann.

Der abschließende Sprachergänzungstest unter G 21 bietet eine Einführung in das breite Spektrum der Aufgaben und Dienstleistungen einer Werbeagentur.

Die Kopiervorlage für den **Progress Check** finden Sie auf **S. 96** in diesem Buch.

LÖSUNGEN

A1 (S. 184)
a. 2; b. 4; c. 7; d. 10; e. 1; f. 5; g. 9; h. 8; i. 3; j. 6

A2 (S. 185)
stand: walls; furnishings: carpet, chairs, display cases, shelves, tables; sales literature: brochures, catalogues, data sheets, leaflets; giveaways: bags, ballpoint pens, key rings; services: catering, cleaning

A3 (S. 185)
possible ideas:
flight and hotel arrangements for sales staff, invitations to customers, shipment of exhibits, shipment of sales literature, design and production of signs, photos, posters

B4 (S. 186)
a. is coming; b. have begun; c. will take place / is taking place; d. has generated; e. have decided; f. are receiving; g. fill; h. send; i. will then be; j. are enclosing / have enclosed / enclose; k. book; l. tend; m. would appreciate; n. could send / would send / sent

B5 (S. 187)
a. form; b. space; c. fee; d. mention; e. supply; f. digital projector; g. at; h. meantime; i. clarified

B6 (S. 188)
Booth size: 3 x 6 m
Preferred location: close to the entrance to the main hall
Furnishings: shelves for the exhibits (1.50 m x 4m x 0.6m), seating for 6 people, dark green carpeting, three large green plants
Technical equipment: halogen lighting, at least five power points (220 V), a security camera and video surveillance
Other services: refreshments (coffee and soft drinks) for the visitors, daily cleaning services

C7 (S. 190)
The one on the right is more effective. It shows the product in use, creates a positive mental picture, shows a person enjoying the product, and suggests that the person seeing the ad will also enjoy the product.

C8 (S. 190)
a. The purpose of advertising is to persuade as many people as possible to buy a company's products or services.
b. The text and design of an advertisement need to be positive and easy to remember.

c. "WIFM" means "what's in it for me", and it means that people want to know how they can benefit by buying or using a product.
d. Some examples of advertising media are television and radio commercials, newspaper and magazine advertisements, billboards, phone calls, direct mail, internet banners, pop-ups and online video commercials.
e. Advertisements need to be created, and air time on the radio and TV and advertising space in newspapers and magazines are expensive.
f. Public relations focuses on the company's image rather than selling specific products or services.

C9 (S. 191)
students' individual ideas

D10 (S. 192)
a. advertising; b. advertisement; c. advertise; d. competitive; e. competitor; f. competition; g. economical; h. economic; i. economize; j. negotiator; k. negotiations; l. negotiable; m. non-negotiable; n. repay; o. payment; p. payee; q. payable

E11 (S. 193)
a, b, d, e, g are appropriate; c, f and h are too direct

E12 (S. 193) CD 1 22
They use g, b, e, and a.

E13 (S. 193) CD 1 22
Dan suggests spending 50% of the advertising budget on trade fairs and 50% on internet advertisements. Mary wants to keep some advertisements in trade magazines and gradually reduce their number.

E14 (S. 193) CD 1 23
students' own answers

E15 (S. 193) CD 1 24
a. Plastics Fair, Düsseldorf; b. Q3900 injection moulding machine; c. Norway; d. grey, dark green, dark blue

E16 (S. 194) CD 1 24
a. F (he wants to make the stand smaller to save money); b. F (the equipment will be brought over from Essen); c. T; d. T; e. T; f. F (they need four power points); g. F (only if they demonstrate the Q3900); h. F (tomorrow)

E17 (S. 194)
individual student performances

F18 (S. 196)

Email

Dear Sir or Madam

Our company is planning to participate in the Household Goods Fair taking place in London from 7 to 10 September this year. For this reason, we would like to book an exhibition stand of 3 x 4 metres. We will require shelves for the exhibits along the back wall as well as two bar-height bistro tables.

Could you please send us a brochure and a floor plan? We would also require the names of reliable companies who install and dismantle stands.

We would appreciate it if you could recommend a hotel for our stay. Is it possible to take public transport to the fair?

Thank you in advance for this information.

Yours sincerely
(Full Name)

G19 (S. 197)

Deutsche Messe AG
Luxemburger Str. 34-38
50674 Köln

22nd January 201_

Mr. Peter Graham
Sales Manager
DownUnder Limited
P.O. Box 2089116
Melbourne, Victoria
Australien

Dear Mr Graham

Your reservation for a stand at the International Food Fair from 25th to 29th April 201_

We are pleased to confirm your reservation for a stand of 3 x 4 metres at this year's International Food Fair in Cologne. You have been assigned stand number 1048, which is located on the 1st level of Hall 7.

››

»

As you requested, the stand will be equipped with the following furnishings: a conference table with four chairs, a kitchenette with hot and cold running water, cups, saucers, plates and glasses, a literature rack, and a lockable display case. Access to electricity, telephone, internet and fax is available. The stand will have dark grey carpeting.

The total price for five days including installation and dismantling of the equipment belonging to the fair amounts to €15,750. Daily cleaning services are included in the price. We would ask you to pay €10,000 in advance and the balance at the beginning of the fair. Please note that the costs for telephone and electricity are to be settled on the last day of the fair.

Please send us your confirmation of these arrangements by email. For your information, we are enclosing a map of Cologne. We look forward to your participation and to a successful fair.

Yours sincerely

Elke Schmied
Exhibits Manager

G20 (S. 197) CD 1 24

Für: Herrn Max Weppner
Verfasst von: Simone Hermann **am:** ....
Gesprächspartner/in: Hilary Gardiner, Londoner Zentrale
Betr.: Bevorstehende Plastikmesse in Düsseldorf

Hilary hat gerade das Handbuch für die Messe bekommen und wollte mit uns die Einzelheiten besprechen. Ihr Chef will aus Kostengründen die Größe des Messestandes auf 3 x 4m reduzieren. Ich wandte ein, dass wir dann unsere Q3900 Spritzgussmaschine nicht ausstellen können. Sie will das noch einmal mit ihrem Chef besprechen.

Was die Ausstattung anbelangt, haben wir uns auf drei Bistro-Stehtische, einen kleinen Konferenztisch und drei Stühle geeinigt. Der Teppichboden soll dieses Mal dunkelblau sein. Wir können unsere eigenen Regale und Schaukästen benutzen. Wir brauchen aber mindestens vier 220V Steckdosen und Internetzugang. Wenn wir den größeren Stand nehmen, um unsere Q3900 zu zeigen, brauchen wir auch Druckluft und fließend kaltes und warmes Wasser.

Da Hilarys Chef erst morgen wieder da ist, gibt sie uns morgen Bescheid, ob wir den größeren Stand buchen sollen.

G21 (S. 198)

The advertising agency

Some large firms **that** use technical advertising have **their** own in-house advertising departments, but the vast majority of manufacturers prefer to outsource **this** service and hire **an** advertising agency. An advertising agency uses different types of media to communicate a sales message **about** a product or service to possible customers. If the message is effective, sales **will** increase. The media chosen will depend on who the possible customers are. Toys and sweets **may** be advertised **during** children's television programmes, for example, **while** technical equipment will probably be advertised in trade journals. No matter **where** the advertisement is placed, the goal is **always** to present the product or service in the **best** possible light so that customers will want to buy **it.**
Some advertising agencies work locally or for a specific branch of industry. Others have staffs of **several** hundred people, work internationally, and handle accounts worth millions of euros. **When** a client starts working **with** an advertising agency, a meeting with an account manager will be arranged. The account manager acts **as** a liaison **between** the client and the rest of the agency. A creative team consisting **of** various specialists will **then** start developing the advertising campaign. Copywriters write the texts of advertisements, **including** slogans and descriptions. Graphic artists design visuals, **such as** logos, pictures or layouts, **which** present the product attractively. Media specialists buy **space** in print media, such as newspapers or magazines, or time slots on broadcast media, such as television or radio, depending on **which** customers they want to reach. During the past **few** years the field of internet advertising has **been** growing **rapidly** as advertising agencies find new ways to reach customers **online.**

UNIT 12
APPLYING FOR JOBS

Content and skills at a glance:

- discussing job preferences
- writing covering letters
- writing a CV (BE) / resume (AE)
- describing personality traits
- handling interview questions

Einleitung

Die Bewerbung gehört eigentlich nicht zum Rahmenstoffplan der IHK-Prüfung *Zusatzqualifikation für Auszubildende Englisch*. Da Bürokräfte mit guten Fremdsprachenkenntnissen sich aber immer öfter bei global agierenden Unternehmen bewerben, bei denen sie einen englischsprachigen Bewerbungsprozess durchlaufen müssen, werden englische Bewerbungen der Vollständigkeit halber an dieser Stelle behandelt. Thematisiert werden die drei wichtigsten Punkte: das Anschreiben, der Lebenslauf und das persönliche Vorstellungsgespräch.

Wichtig ist, dass zwischen einem deutschen Lebenslauf und einem auf Englisch abgefassten *CV* bzw. *resume* deutliche Unterschiede bestehen. Auf diese Unterschiede sowie auf die unterschiedlichen Schulabschlüsse wird konkret hingewiesen.

Auf das persönliche Vorstellungsgespräch kann und sollte man sich grundsätzlich vorbereiten. Absatz E liefert praktische Hinweise für eine solche Vorbereitung und erläutert mögliche Fragen, die in einem Vorstellungsgespräch gestellt werden könnten.

Den Abschluss dieses Lehrwerks bilden auf Englisch abgefasste Stellenanzeigen unter F 18, die in dieser Form auch in einer englischsprachigen Zeitung erscheinen könnten.

Die Kopiervorlage für den **Progress Check** finden Sie auf **S. 97** in diesem Buch.

LÖSUNGEN

A1 / A2 (S. 201)

students' individual answers

B3 (S. 202)

a. 2; b. 1; c. 2; d. 3; e. 1; f. 2; g. 3

B4 (S. 203)

a. day-to-day; b. enquiries; c. delivery; d. needed; e. professional; f. native; g. experience; h. pressure

B5 (S. 204)

a. saw; b. match; c. would like; d. have worked / have been working; e. has taught; f. joined; g. was given; h. allows; i. has been; j. would like

C6 (S. 205)

suggested answers

a. Layout and structure: The LL has the heading "Lebenslauf" at the top; the CV starts with the name. The LL includes a photo; headings for the personal information; and the date and the signature of the applicant. The CV doesn't include these items. The information on the LL is lined up along the left-hand margin; some of the information on the CV is centered on the page.

b. Personal information: The personal information on the LL is more detailed, including date of birth, place of birth, family status and nationality. (A CV can include date of birth and nationality, but they are not required.)

c. Education: The LL includes primary school; the CV starts with secondary school. The LL uses chronological order, while the CV uses reverse chronological order.

d. Work experience: The LL has a special category for the apprenticeship; on the CV, this is listed under "Work experience" because apprenticeships aren't as common in English-speaking countries as in Germany. The CV includes more detailed descriptions of responsibilities; each description starts with an active verb. The LL uses chronological order, while the CV uses reverse chronological order.

e. Language and skills: Different layout, but otherwise very similar. The CV lists typing speed as "words per minute", whereas the LL lists typing speed as "characters per minute" ("Anschläge pro Minute").

f. Interests and activities: No differences.

g. References: The LL doesn't mention references because copies of references and school certificates will be sent with the application. The CV makes a general statement: "References are available on request" ("Referenzen erhältlich auf Anfrage").

C7 (S. 208)
The points that describe her responsibilites each start with an active verb. She uses present tense for her current job and past tense for jobs she used to have.

C8 (S. 209)
a. coordinated appointments; b. handled business correspondence; c. processed and monitored orders; d. checked and sent export documents; e. organized trade fair participation; f. planned trips (booked hotels, flights, rental cars) g. visited customers throughout Europe

D9 (S. 209)
a. multi-tasker; b. team player; c. troubleshooter; d. leader; e. self-starter

D10 (S. 209)
a. motivated; b. flexible; c. outgoing; d. creative; e. supportive; f. reliable; g. organized; *extra adjective:* persuasive

D11 (S. 210)
students' individual answers

E12 (S. 210)
a. J; b. P; c. B; d. P; e. P; f. J; g. P; h. B; i. J; j. J

E13 (S. 210)/**E14** (S. 211)
students' individual answers

E15 (S. 211) CD 1 25
a. 2; b. 2; c. 3; d. 1; e. 3

E16 (S. 211) CD 1 26
a. Do you offer opportunities for training and professional development?
b. Could you describe a typical day for someone in this position?
c. What gives this company an advantage over its competitors?
d. How often would my performance be evaluated?
e. When can I expect to hear from you?

E17 (S. 212)/**F18**/**F19** (S. 214/215)
individual student performances/work

KOPIERVORLAGEN
PROGRESS CHECKS

Die nachfolgenden Kopiervorlagen wurden auf dem Format DinA-4 erstellt und erscheinen hier aufgrund des Buchformats in verkleinerter Form.

Wenn Sie die Kopiervorlagen für Ihren Unterricht vorbereiten, benutzen Sie den Zoomfaktor 125%, um sie auf DinA-4 Format zu vergrößern.

Die Lösungen zu diesen Aufgaben finden Sie im Anhang.

UNIT 1 OPEN FOR BUSINESS

1 Formal and informal style

Decide if the following sentences belong in a formal letter or an informal email.
Then, on a separate sheet of paper, rearrange the sentences and write the email and the letter.

	formal	informal
a. Dear Mr Blackstone	☐	☐
b. Dear Sheila	☐	☐
c. As I am planning to be in Glasgow next week, I was wondering if I might stop by your office to introduce you to our latest line of all-natural shampoo.	☐	☐
d. Customer response to this product has been overwhelmingly positive.	☐	☐
e. Looking forward to seeing you soon!	☐	☐
f. I am looking forward to meeting you.	☐	☐
g. I will phone your office by the end of the week to find out when would be a convenient time.	☐	☐
h. I'll also bring along a couple of samples of our new shampoo.	☐	☐
i. Just wanted to let you know that I'll be in Glasgow next week; do you want to have lunch?	☐	☐
j. Of course, I would also bring several samples for you and your staff to test.	☐	☐
k. Our customers love it!	☐	☐
l. Perhaps we could arrange a meeting for Thursday or Friday.	☐	☐
m. Cheers	☐	☐
n. Tuesday or Wednesday would be great for me; just pick the day and let me know.	☐	☐
o. Yours sincerely	☐	☐

2 Welcoming visitors

Put the following words in the right order to create sentences.

a. help / how / I / may / you

-- ?

b. a / afraid / at / I'm / in / meeting / moment / she's / the

-- .

c. can / drink / I / offer / something / to / you

-- ?

d. I'd / introduce / like / manager / our / sales / to / to / you

-- .

e. meet / pleased / to / you

-- .

UNIT 2 GETTING IN CONTACT

1 Writing enquiries

Some of the sentences contain a grammar mistake. Tick the sentences that are correct.
Cross out the mistakes in the incorrect sentences and write the correct forms in the blank.

a. We are seeing your advertisement in last month's issue of Hydraulics Today. ________________
b. Your company was recommended to us from one of our business associates. ________________
c. Send us please your latest catalogue. ________________
d. We would appreciate receiving a quotation for your Silver 500 knife set. ________________
e. If possible, we like to receive some samples of your products. ________________
f. We look forward to hear from you soon. ________________

2 Telephoning

Fill in the blanks in the following phone conversations.

A: Good morning, Burke Limited. How can I (a) ________________ you?
B: This is Sabine Schütt calling from Weißenfeld GmbH in Berlin, Germany.
Could I (b) ________________ to Denise Kingston, please?
A: I'm sorry, she's (c) ________________ of the office at the moment. (d) ________________ I take a message?
B: Yes, that (e) ________________ be very nice.
My name is Sabine Schütt and I'm with Weißenfeld GmbH in Berlin.
A: Could you (f) ________________ your name for me, please?
B: Certainly. It's S as in Sam, A-B-I-N-E, last name S-C-H-U-E (g) ________________ T as in Tom.
A: OK, I've got it. Could you (h) ________________ the company name? I didn't quite get it the first time.
B: Sure. It's Weißenfeld GmbH, capital W-E-I-double S-E-N-F-E-L-D, G-M-B-H.
A: And your message?
B: My flight time has been changed and I'll be an hour late to our meeting this afternoon. In case there's a problem, she (i) ________________ phone me. My number's 49 for Germany, 157 880 7969.
A: I'll (j) ________________ that back to you: it's 157 880 769.
B: Almost! It's 157 880 7969.
A: Right. Now I've got it. I'll (k) ________________ her the message as (l) ________________ as she returns.
B: Thanks very much. Good-bye.
A: Thank you for calling. Good-bye.

UNIT 3 MAKING OFFERS

1 Terminology related to offers

Fill in the crossword puzzle with the English translations of the German terms.

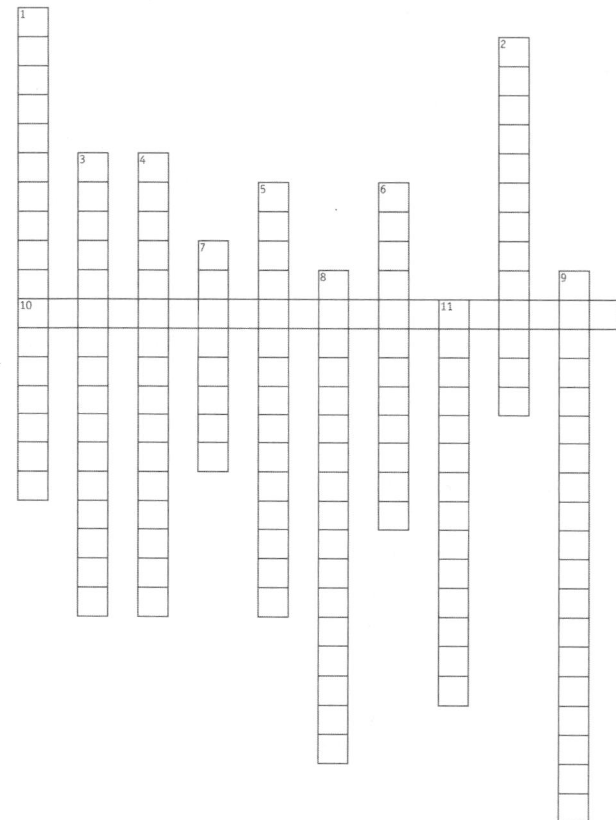

Across

10. Erstauftragsrabatt

Down

1. Großhandelsrabatt
2. Händlerrabatt
3. Mengenrabatt
4. unverlangtes Angebot
5. Exportpreisliste
6. Skonto
7. Gültigkeit
8. Vorbehaltsklausel
9. Einführungsrabatt
11. verlangtes Angebot

2 Writing offers

Match the beginnings a.–h. with the endings 1.–8. to make complete sentences.

a. We are confident that
b. Our delivery period is
c. Please note that
d. The prices are quoted
e. We are enclosing
f. Many thanks for
g. We are delighted to hear that
h. Please refer to

1. you are interested in our products.
2. a sample of our tea.
3. your enquiry about our range of pens.
4. the attached price list for details.
5. usually two to three weeks.
6. EXW Bremen.
7. you will be impressed by the quality of our products.
8. we are willing to grant a quantity discount of 5%.

UNIT 4 PLACING ORDERS

1 Incoterms® 2010

Complete the grid with the following words.

alongside | board | carriage | carrier | cost | duty | freight | freight | insurance | insurance | place | terminal | works

EXW	Ex (a) ________________	DDP	Delivered (g) ________________ paid
FCA	Free (b) ________________	FAS	Free (h) ________________ ship
CPT	(c) ________________ paid to	FOB	Free on (i) ________________
CIP	Carriage and (d) ________________ paid to	CFR	(j) ________________ and (k) ________________
DAT	Delivered at (e) ________________	CIF	Cost, (l) ________________ and (m) ________________
DAP	Delivered at (f) ________________		

2 Writing orders

Put the following words in the right order to create sentences.

a. 13 / for / many / May / of / offer / thanks / your

____.

b. are / by / impressed / of / quality / samples / the / we / your

____.

c. following / in / order / placing / pleasure / take / the / we / with / you

____.

d. agreed / as / bank / by / effect / payment / transfer / we / will

____.

e. be / DAP / is / Jena / price / the / to / understood

____.

f. are / care / ensure / goods / packed / please / that / the / the / utmost / with

____.

g. forward / goods / in / look / receiving / the / time / to / we

____.

UNIT 5 DEALING WITH ORDERS

1 Payment vocabulary

Translate the following expressions into English.
Then find each English expression in the word search grid.

a Zahlungsziel ________________________________
b Bankscheck ________________________________
c Überweisung ________________________________
d Wechsel ________________________________
e Barzahlung bei Auftragserteilung ______________
f Scheck ________________________________
g Kreditkarte ________________________________
h Rabatt ________________________________
i Raten ________________________________
j Rechnung ________________________________
k Akkreditiv ________________________________
l rein netto ________________________________

	A	B	C	D	E	F	G	H	I	J	K	L	M	N	O
1	h	t	u	z	r	l	n	e	f	b	r	b	l	g	b
2	b	n	m	l	u	i	c	l	k	i	e	s	k	i	a
3	a	u	t	p	t	i	m	e	f	l	d	m	m	n	n
4	r	o	n	k	o	o	x	x	k	l	r	r	n	s	k
5	l	c	f	v	z	h	s	z	h	o	o	e	x	t	t
6	q	s	n	g	p	s	d	a	r	f	h	t	v	a	r
7	t	i	d	e	r	c	f	o	r	e	t	t	e	l	a
8	c	d	c	h	e	q	u	e	n	x	i	n	d	m	n
9	d	r	a	c	t	i	d	e	r	c	w	u	q	e	s
10	h	g	f	v	u	v	q	l	n	h	h	o	g	n	f
11	y	h	c	l	u	p	x	c	t	a	s	c	w	t	e
12	l	p	j	d	v	g	b	d	s	n	a	c	z	s	r
13	w	e	k	v	a	x	y	f	x	g	c	a	l	b	b
14	s	t	r	i	c	t	l	y	n	e	t	h	w	p	j
15	b	a	n	k	e	r	s	d	r	a	f	t	s	s	y

2 Writing order confirmations

Unscramble the words to find synonyms for the underlined expressions.

a. We will do our best to <u>speed up</u> the completion of your order. (XETIEDPE) ________________________________
b. Your order will be handled <u>quickly</u>. (YMOPPLTR) ________________________________
c. Your order is now being <u>worked on</u> (DSCEPROES) ________________________________ and should be ready for <u>shipment</u> (HTDCPSAI) in the next few days. ________________________________
d. <u>Better</u> terms of payment can be offered to regular customers. (EOMR ALBEFORUVA) ________________________________
e. We <u>are sorry</u> that the item you ordered is no longer available. (ERTEGR) ________________________________

UNIT 6 ORGANIZING TRANSPORT

1 Sentences related to transport

Match the beginnings a.–h. with the endings 1.–8. to make complete sentences.

a. The goods you ordered on 5 December
b. The consignment was handed over
c. The goods have been loaded
d. As requested, the goods have been
e. The documents will be released to you
f. We trust that the goods will
g. The MS Ocean Wings is due to arrive
h. The packages have been marked

1. on board the MS Atlantic Light.
2. packed with the utmost care.
3. on acceptance of our 30-day sight draft.
4. in Singapore on or about 23 March.
5. are now ready for dispatch.
6. "Fragile".
7. arrive punctually and in good condition.
8. to the freight forwarder yesterday.

2 Shipping documents

Unscramble each of the expressions. Copy the letters in the numbered cells to other cells with the same number to find out the solution.

LILWAYB — 4
LILB FO LIDGNA — 10 3
NGCIPAK SITL — 9
COLRCAMMEI VIINOEC — 12 2
TIECECRIFTA FO ROGIIN — 5 11
RUINEANSC RACCEFTIITE — 7
XEPTOR LEICECN — 8
RIA WIBLALY — 1 6

H _ _ _ _ _ (1 2 3 4 5) _ _ _ H (6 7 8) _ _ _ _ (9 10 11 12)

UNIT 7 REQUESTING PAYMENT

1 Payment reminders

Underline the correct expression.

a. Enclosed you will find our invoice in the *quantity / amount* of €6,800.
b. Please *remit / settle* this amount to our account within 30 days.
c. We *write / are writing* to let you know about a problem with your payment.
d. Payment of our invoice is *now / yet* four weeks overdue.
e. We would *require / request* that you pay this invoice without delay.
f. In case you have already paid, please *ignore / forget* this letter.
g. Thank you in advance for your *collaboration / cooperation*.

2 Discussing payment problems

Rewrite this conversation to make it more polite.

A: Helen Huber, Accounts Department.
(a) This is Helen Huber, Accounts Department. Can I help you? ________________
B: My name is Clark Wagner from Labels Plus. I am very angry.
(b) ________________
A: Why?
(c) ________________
B: You haven't paid our invoice.
(d) ________________
A: You're wrong. We have.
(e) ________________
B: Then why haven't I received payment?
(f) ________________
A: We paid by bank transfer yesterday.
(g) ________________
B: But the invoice was due two weeks ago.
(h) ________________
A: I know, but we couldn't pay then.
(i) ________________
B: You should have told me.
(j) ________________
A: Sorry.
(k) ________________
B: Well, don't let it happen again!
(l) ________________
A: OK. Good-bye.
(m) ________________
B: Good-bye.
(n) ________________

UNIT 8 REDUCING RISKS

1 Writing credit enquiries

Put the following words in the right order to create sentences.

a. a / as / been / by / given / have / name / reference / S+K GmbH / we / your

---.

b. a / company / customer / is / long-time / of / this / yours

---?

c. any / be / could / for / grateful / information / provide / we / would / you

---.

d. any / completely / confidential / information / provide / remain / will / you

---.

e. advance / assistance / for / in / thank / you / your

---.

2 Responding to credit enquiries

Put the verbs into the correct form.

a. The company you asked about ---------------- (be) a regular customer of ours for several years.
b. We are pleased to report that they always ---------------- (pay) their invoices punctually.
c. Unfortunately, the company in question ---------------- (experience) some financial difficulties at the moment.
d. Recently they ---------------- (lose) several important customers.
e. In order to collect payment, we ---------------- (have) to initiate legal proceedings against them last month.
f. We would now only deliver to them if payment ---------------- (is) made in advance.
g. We trust that this information ---------------- (be) handled in strict confidence.

3 Shipping vocabulary

Do these expressions refer to transport by sea, rail or road? Write each one next to the correct category:

capsize | derail | harbour | lorry | motorway | pier | port | ship |
speed limit | station | tracks | traffic jam | train | truck

a. Sea

b. Rail

c. Road

UNIT 9 HANDLING COMPLAINTS

1 Writing letters of complaint

Unscramble the words to find synonyms for the underlined expressions.

a. We took delivery of (EVCRIEDE) our order no. 2498 yesterday and regret to inform you that there is cause (AONSRE) for complaint. ________________
b. On inspecting (NGEMNIIAX) the shipment we saw (CNTDOIE) that one of the boxes was missing. ________________
c. For your information, we are enclosing a list of the missing items. (RLCATSIE) ________________
d. Apparently an error (a SKEMTAI) was made when the goods were packed. ________________
e. We are only willing to keep the damaged goods if you lower (DCUREE) the price by 50%. ________________
f. Please let us know when we can expect delivery of the delayed shipment. (ONNTGSNCMEI) ________________
g. We trust that we will receive your answer (SPENEORS) in the very near future. ________________

2 Responding to letters of complaint

Write the correct preposition in each blank.

a. We are sorry to hear ________ the problems you are having ________ your order no. 736521.
b. We are looking ________ this matter and will be ________ touch soon to let you know what we have found ________ .
c. Our packing department did not take sufficient care ________ the packing ________ your order.
d. The details ________ your order were entered ________ our computer system incorrectly.
e. Our freight forwarders have located your shipment. It is expected to reach you ________ the end of the week ________ the latest.
f. Replacements ________ the damaged articles are already ________ their way ________ you.
g. We are prepared to grant you a 40% discount ________ the list price.
h. We will do our best to resolve this matter ________ a way which is satisfactory ________ both ________ us.
i. You may wish to take ________ this matter ________ your insurance company.

UNIT 10 TRAVELLING FOR BUSINESS

1 Making a hotel reservation

Fill in the blanks in the following phone conversations.

A: Courtbridge Suites of Maple Grove. (a) ______________ is Doreen. How can I help you?

B: Hello, my name is Konrad Eigner and I'd like to (b) ______________ a reservation.

A: Certainly. When would you (c) ______________ to stay with us?

B: I'll be (d) ______________ in Maple Grove on October 4th and staying for at least three weeks while I'm working at a customer's office there.

A: I see. Well, that shouldn't be a problem at all. We've got several suites (e) ______________ . Is the reservation just for yourself?

B: Yes, it is.

A: Then I suppose you'll want our one-bedroom suite including a seating area with a widescreen (f) ______________ , a small kitchen and a bathroom. The (g) ______________ for that would be $129 per night.

B: What services are included?

A: We've got a 24-hour business center with a computer, printer, scanner and fax. High-speed wireless (h) ______________ access is available throughout the hotel. We also have a fitness room and an indoor swimming (i) ______________ .

B: That sounds good. Does the kitchen have everything I need in order to cook?

A: Yes, it's fully (j) ______________ with everything from pots and pans to plates and cutlery. The rate also (k) ______________ a buffet breakfast with a range of hot and cold items.

B: Excellent.

A: So, can I go ahead and make the (l) ______________ for you?

B: Yes, please. Once again, my name is Konrad Eigner, K-O-N-R-A-D E-I-G-N-E-R. Do you (m) ______________ my credit card number?

A: Yes, to guarantee the reservation.

B: It's a MasterCard, 4300 9779 2378 3046.

A: Right, I've got it. I'll put you down for three weeks for now. If you could give us three days' notice before checking out, that would be great.

B: Of course. Well, thank you very much.

A: My pleasure. Thank you for (n) ______________

2 Vocabulary for talking about companies

Underline the correct expression.

a. The money a company earns after paying its expenses is the *capital / profit*.
b. In the US, the head of a company is often called the *managing director / CEO*.
c. A *shareholder / creditor* is someone to whom money is owed.
d. PLCs are *privately held / publicly traded* companies.
e. "Inc." stands for *incorporation / incorporated*.

UNIT 11 EXHIBITING AT TRADE FAIRS

1 Trade fair vocabulary

Translate the following expressions into English. Then find each English expression in the word search grid.

a. Gang ______________________

b. (Messe-)Besucher/in ______________________

c. Theke ______________________

d. Schaukasten ______________________

e. Ausstellungsstück ______________________

f. Aussteller ______________________

g. Bodenfläche ______________________

h. Werbegeschenke ______________________

i. Erfrischungen ______________________

j. Verkaufsmaterial ______________________

k. Vertriebsmitarbeiter/in ______________________

____

	A	B	C	D	E	F	G	H	I	J	K	L	M	N	O
1	s	h	s	u	e	z	a	e	e	b	w	d	r	r	s
2	h	a	l	y	r	x	e	j	c	p	i	o	e	o	f
3	l	g	l	x	a	d	h	n	r	s	g	y	f	t	f
4	m	r	m	e	n	w	a	i	p	j	s	c	r	i	y
5	y	l	o	e	s	i	a	l	b	p	o	o	e	b	e
6	y	a	t	y	s	l	a	e	h	i	b	u	s	i	p
7	w	t	b	l	k	y	i	x	v	g	t	n	h	h	h
8	a	u	e	l	c	k	o	t	y	i	l	t	m	x	p
9	q	u	s	a	l	e	s	r	e	p	g	e	e	e	u
10	w	e	s	t	p	u	r	o	n	r	c	r	n	r	w
11	u	e	y	h	t	f	u	v	q	n	a	g	t	r	n
12	e	c	a	p	s	r	o	o	l	f	v	t	s	q	r
13	g	s	g	m	e	a	f	g	e	j	m	q	u	o	r
14	e	z	t	z	y	r	q	o	y	b	q	c	p	r	q
15	w	o	d	g	j	t	v	q	x	l	b	b	s	y	e

2 Word building

Find appropriate forms and complete the table.

Verb	Noun	Noun (person)	Adjective
compete	(a)	(b)	competitive
(c)	advertising (d)	advertiser	advertised
negotiate	(e)	(f)	negotiable
(g)	payment	payee	(h)
economize	(i)	economist	economical (j)

UNIT 12 APPLYING FOR JOBS

1 Positive personalities

Unscramble each of the expressions. Copy the letters in the numbered cells to other cells with the same number to find out the solution.

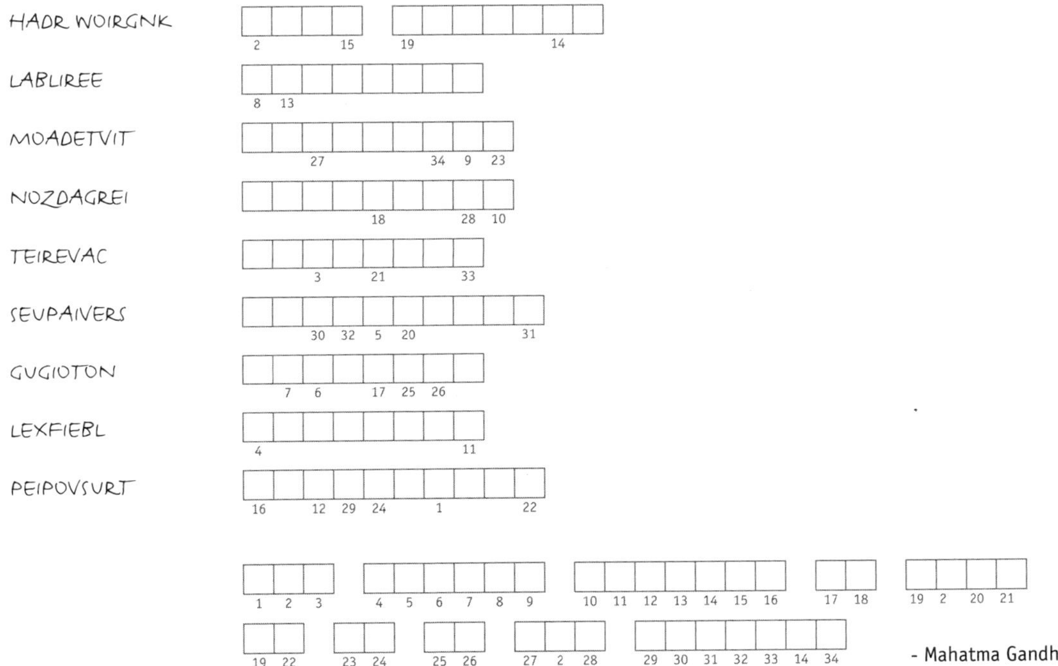

- Mahatma Gandhi

2 Writing a covering letter

Match the beginnings a.–h. with the endings 1.–8. to make complete sentences.

a. I am experienced
b. Not only am I a reliable worker, I can also adapt easily
c. Please let me know if I can provide
d. I hope to be able to make
e. My language skills would certainly help me communicate
f. I would welcome
g. My background closely matches
h. I am keen to take on

1. to new situations.
2. the opportunity to discuss this position with you in person.
3. a valuable contribution to the success of your company.
4. the requirements described in the advertisement.
5. you with any further information.
6. with your international customers.
7. some new and exciting challenges.
8. in processing orders for export.

LÖSUNGEN – PROGRESS CHECKS

UNIT 1

1 *formal:* a, c, d, f, g, j, l, o; *informal:* b, e, h, i, k, m, n

Formal letter

> Dear Mr Blackstone
>
> As I am planning to be in Glasgow next week, I was wondering if I might stop by your office to introduce you to our latest line of all-natural shampoo. Customer response to this product has been overwhelmingly positive. Of course, I would also be pleased to bring several samples for you and your staff to test.
>
> Perhaps we could arrange a meeting for Thursday or Friday. I will phone your office by the end of the week to find out when would be a convenient time. I am looking forward to meeting you.
>
> Yours sincerely

Informal email

> **Email**
>
> Dear Sheila
>
> Just wanted to let you know that I'll be in Glasgow next week; do you want to have lunch? I'll also bring you a couple samples of our fantastic new shampoo. Our customers love it!
>
> Tuesday or Wednesday would be great for me; just pick the day and let me know. Looking forward to seeing you soon!
>
> Cheers

2 a. How may I help you? b. I'm afraid she's in a meeting at the moment. c. Can I offer you something to drink? d. I'd like to introduce you to our sales manager. e. Pleased to meet you.

UNIT 2

1 a. ~~are seeing~~ → saw; b. of → by; c. ~~Send us please~~ → Please send us; d. correct; e. ~~we like~~ → we would like; f. ~~to hear~~ → to hearing

2 a. help; b. speak, talk; c. out; d. May, Can; e. would; f. spell; g. double; h. repeat; i. can, should; j. read, repeat; k. give, leave; l. soon

UNIT 3

1 Across: 10. initial order discount
Down: 1. wholesale discount, 2. trade discount, 3. quantity discount, 4. unsolicited offer, 5. export price list, 6. cash discount, 7. validity, 8. reservation clause, 9. introductory discount, 11. solicited offer

2 a. 7; b. 5; c. 8; d. 6; e. 2; f. 3; g. 1; h. 4

UNIT 4

1 a. works; b. carrier; c. Carriage; d. insurance; e. terminal; f. place; g. duty; h. alongside; i. board; j. cost; k. freight; l. insurance; m. freight

2 a. Many thanks for your offer of 13 May. b. We are impressed by the quality of your samples. c. We take pleasure in placing the following order with you: d. As agreed we will effect payment by bank transfer. e. The price is to be understood DAP Jena. f. Please ensure that the goods are packed with the utmost care. g. We look forward to receiving the goods in time.

UNIT 5

1 Use the letter and number grid to find the first letter of each expression.
a. account terms (L, 13)
b. banker's draft (A, 15)
c. bank transfer (O, 1)
d. bill of exchange (J, 1)
e. cash with order (K, 13)
f. cheque (C, 8)
g. credit card (J, 9)
h. discount (B, 8)
i. instalments (N, 2)
j. invoice (B, 7)
k. letter of credit (N, 7)
l. strictly net (A, 14)

	A	B	C	D	E	F	G	H	I	J	K	L	M	N	O
1	h	t	u	z	r	l	n	e	f	b	r	b	l	g	b
2	b	n	m	l	u	i	c	l	k	i	e	s	k	i	a
3	a	u	t	p	t	i	m	e	f	l	d	m	m	n	n
4	r	o	n	k	o	o	x	x	k	l	r	r	n	s	k
5	l	c	f	v	z	h	s	z	h	o	o	e	x	t	t
6	q	s	n	g	p	s	d	a	r	f	h	t	v	a	r
7	t	i	d	e	r	c	f	o	r	e	t	t	e	l	a
8	c	d	c	h	e	q	u	e	n	x	i	n	d	m	n
9	d	r	a	c	t	i	d	e	r	c	w	u	q	e	s
10	h	g	f	v	u	v	q	l	n	h	h	o	g	n	f
11	y	h	c	l	u	p	x	c	t	a	s	c	w	t	e
12	l	p	j	d	v	g	b	d	s	n	a	c	z	s	r
13	w	e	k	v	a	x	y	f	x	g	c	a	l	b	b
14	s	t	r	i	c	t	l	y	n	e	t	h	w	p	j
15	b	a	n	k	e	r	s	d	r	a	f	t	s	s	y

2 a. expedite; b. promptly; c. processed, dispatch; d. more favourable; e. regret

UNIT 6

1 a. 5; b. 8; c. 1; d. 2; e. 3; f. 7; g. 4; h. 6

2 a. waybill; b. bill of lading; c. packing list; d. commercial invoice; e. certificate of origin; f. insurance certificate; g. export licence; h. air waybill, *solution:* handle with care

UNIT 7

1 a. amount; b. remit; c. are writing; d. now; e. request; f. ignore; g. cooperation

2 (One of many possible solutions)

a. Helen: This is Helen Huber, Accounts Department. Can I help you?

b. Clark: This is Clark Wagner from Labels Plus. Unfortunately I need to talk to you about a problem.

c. Helen: What seems to be the trouble?

d. Clark: According to our records our latest invoice hasn't been paid yet.

e. Helen: Actually, we have already paid that invoice.

f. Clark: Well, we haven't received payment yet. Do you have any idea why that might be?

g. Helen: We just paid by bank transfer yesterday, and I suppose it will take a few days for the money to reach your account.

h. Clark: Yesterday? That's good to hear, but in fact the invoice was due two weeks ago.

i. Helen: Yes, I know, but we had some difficulties here and unfortunately weren't able to pay the invoice.

j. Clark: I wish you had told me. I'm sure we could have worked something out.

k. Helen: I do apologize for the inconvenience.

l. Clark: Well, I'm glad we've got the situation figured out. If something like this happens in the future, please do let me know.

m. Helen: I certainly will. Thanks for understanding. Good-bye.

n. Clark: Have a good day. Good-bye.

UNIT 8

1 a. We have been given your name as a reference by Schmidt+Kogel GmbH. b. Is this company a long-time customer of yours? c. We would be grateful for any information you could provide. d. Any information you provide will remain completely confidential. e. Thank you in advance for your assistance.

2 a. has been; b. pay; c. is experiencing / are experiencing; d. have lost; e. had; f. were / was; g. will be

3 a. capsize, harbour, pier, port, ship; b. derail, station, tracks, train; c. lorry, motorway, speed limit, traffic jam, truck

UNIT 9

1 a. received, reason; b. examining, noticed; c. articles; d. a mistake; e. reduce; f. consignment; g. response

2 a. about, with; b. into, in, out; c. with, of; d. of, into; e. by, at; f. for, on, to; g. off / on; h. in, for, of; i. up, with

UNIT 10

1 a. This; b. make; c. like; d. arriving; e. available; f. TV, television; g. rate, price; h. internet; i. pool; j. equipped; k. includes; l. reservation, booking; m. need; n. calling, phoning, ringing

2 a. profit; b. CEO; c. creditor; d. publicly traded; e. incorporated

UNIT 11

1 Use the letter and number grid to find the first letter of each expression.

a. aisle (G, 4)
b. attendee (A, 8)
c. counter (L, 4)
d. display case (L, 1)
e. exhibit (E, 1)
f. exhibitor (N, 9)
g. floor space (J, 12)
h. giveaways (K, 9)
i. refreshments (M, 1)
j. sales literature (A, 1)
k. sales rep (C, 9)

	A	B	C	D	E	F	G	H	I	J	K	L	M	N	O
1	s	h	s	u	e	z	a	e	e	b	w	d	r	r	s
2	h	a	l	y	r	x	e	j	c	p	i	o	e	o	f
3	l	g	l	x	a	d	h	n	r	s	g	y	f	t	f
4	m	r	m	e	n	w	a	i	p	j	s	c	r	i	y
5	y	l	o	e	s	i	a	l	b	p	o	o	e	b	e
6	y	a	t	y	s	l	a	e	h	i	b	u	s	i	p
7	w	t	b	l	k	y	i	x	v	g	t	n	h	h	h
8	a	u	e	l	c	k	o	t	y	i	l	t	m	x	p
9	q	u	s	a	l	e	s	r	e	p	g	e	e	e	u
10	w	e	s	t	p	u	r	o	n	r	c	r	n	r	w
11	u	e	y	h	t	f	u	v	q	n	a	g	t	r	n
12	e	c	a	p	s	r	o	o	l	f	v	t	s	q	r
13	g	s	g	m	e	a	f	g	e	j	m	q	u	o	r
14	e	z	t	z	y	r	q	o	y	b	q	c	p	r	q
15	w	o	d	g	j	t	v	q	x	l	b	b	s	y	e

2 a. competition; b. competitor; c. advertise; d. advertisement; e. negotiation; f. negotiator; g. pay; h. payable; i. economics; j. economic

UNIT 12

1 a. hard-working; b. reliable; c. motivated; d. organized; e. creative; f. persuasive; g. outgoing; h. flexible; i. supportive, *solution:* The future depends on what we do in the present.

2 a. 8; b. 1; c. 5; d. 3; e. 6; f. 2; g. 4; h. 7.